Grace in the Garden:
Thirty Years
of
Blunders and Bliss

Grace Peterson

ALL THINGS

THAT MATTER
PRESS

Grace in the Garden: Thirty Years of Blunders and Bliss

ISBN: 978-0-9960413-0-0

Library of Congress Control Number: 2014936590

Cover Photo: Lupine 'Gallery Red' stands watch over William Baffin rose on a bright July day, by Grace Peterson.

To my four budding progeny
and
their faithful father.

A garden is always a series of losses set against a few triumphs, like life itself.

~May Sarton (1912-1995)
American poet, novelist, and memoirist

Table of Contents

Introduction

My first real garden took shape in the summer of 1984. I say *real* because there were a few somewhat halfhearted dress rehearsals before the big debut. And to be honest, the big debut wasn't all that impressive.

The first rehearsal happened in the spring of 1979 when my sister and I were sharing an apartment on the outskirts of northeast Portland, Oregon. In my mind, the area is infamously known for one thing: the East Wind. Driven by a bizarre meteorological force, the East Wind is an icy malevolence that originates in Siberia—or the polar ice cap or some obscure tundra. It picks up speed as it travels south, then funnels through the picturesque Columbia River Gorge. Eventually, at speeds often topping forty miles per hour, it pummels its frigid venom on the outlying areas of Portland and the municipalities known as Troutdale, Wood Village, and Gresham.

As I trudged eastward to Reynolds High School during my senior year, I was assaulted by the angry East Wind as it spewed its unrelenting bluster across my exposed face and weaseled its way through my inadequate layers of clothing. I harbored just enough defiance to propel me forward towards graduating—and a future. I'm pretty sure I looked like death as I entered the Senior Building bathroom to wipe my snotty nose and the mascara smear from my frozen face.

Still in survival mode as a result of our childhood traumas, my sister and I had come together to pool our resources after several years of going our separate ways. We still had our issues, carrying unhealed wounds incurred by ignorant and selfish caregivers. Despite our bickering, we shared a mutual love of gardening. When spring came and the East Wind finally went on hiatus, we raked away a spot of the bark dust that lined the edge of our concrete patio and dug a hole big enough for the cherry tomato plant we'd picked up on a whim while buying groceries. With nary a clue as to how to care for the little thing, we sat back and watched, ignorant but hopeful.

As mysteriously as Jack's beanstalk reached towards the heavens, our tomato plant morphed overnight from its humble beginnings into something otherworldly, towering over our heads, with glistening red globes hanging in delectable clusters.

I remember wondering if there was some kind of radioactive ingredient in the soil to cause such a transformation, like on *Gilligan's*

Island when they grew all those enormous veggies. Or maybe it was just beginner's luck.

A few years later, on the wings of the tomato plant anomaly and perhaps fueled by a smidgen of the gardening DNA passed down from my paternal grandparents, I dug out a strip of lawn along the façade of the apartment building where my husband Steve and I lived. I purchased several blooming marigold plants and lined them up like obedient soldiers. I tucked them into the weedy soil and told them to grow.

Marigolds and roses were the only two flowers I could properly identify back in 1980. I had so much to learn. Perhaps Madeline, the elderly lady who lived upstairs, knew this and was channeling my grandparents. Often while I was watering or weeding, she'd pop her head out of her window and holler her encouragement down at me. She'd invite me up for coffee and, while I nuzzled her friendly cat, complain about the apartment managers and their refusal to beautify the grounds. She'd tell me how much she appreciated my efforts.

Madeline's tiny two-bedroom apartment contained an entire houseful of furniture. I suppose she was a hoarder of sorts, but the messiness normally associated with that dysfunction wasn't there. Her apartment was indeed cramped, but was also exceptionally tidy. I believe she revealed a reason for all the furniture, but I can't recall what it was. What I do remember was the painting that hung on the wall in her spare bedroom. Given that my preferences had up until then leaned towards the outdoors with botanical or nature scenes, I was surprised at my own reaction when I saw this fabulous piece of artwork.

Like looking through a portal to a bygone era, British maidens were dressed to the nines in their 19th century finery, attending what must have been some type of debutante ball in a lavishly decorated ballroom. My affection for Madeline's painting was rather haunting. I thought about it long after trekking back downstairs to my own digs. Secretly, I wished that Madeline would offer it to me. I didn't have the nerve to ask if I could buy it from her. The painting seemed too sacred and my desire for it felt like sacrilege. Although I'm not a romantic, I held on to this romantic image of wispy, flouncy pastels and toyed with how to make it a reality in my modern world.

I'm sure Madeline had no idea how her simple words of encouragement fed my hungry soul. I wasn't familiar with affirmations from the older generation, especially for what seemed like such a small thing as planting a row of Marigolds. But her sweet words were a rare gift.

***

My paternal grandparents were talented, hard working people and it showed in everything they did, most especially the idyllic landscape they created and tended that bordered the tranquil flow of the North Umpqua River in southern Oregon. An oval, central lawn was surrounded by plants I much later would identify as Azaleas in spring and Asters and Black-Eyed Susans in summer. Just to the right of the lawn was a gigantic vegetable and fruit garden surrounded by a tall fence to keep the deer out. My grandma's preserved green beans were ambrosia even to a fussy eater like me.

My siblings were equally enchanted with our grandparents' property. We all loved being there, hunting for frogs in the creek, making forts. Sometimes I'd traipse off alone and, when I was sure no one was watching, I'd saunter down the gravel path singing like the ladies on TV's variety shows. *Would you like to ride in my beautiful balloon ...?*

My father and mother must have loved the grandparents' property, too, because when I was six years old, they purchased river property a few miles downstream and built a big house. The rural subdivision, called Echo Bend, had only a few houses dotting the grassy lots. Although my parents were unable for a variety of reasons to create a garden, it didn't matter. The indigenous landscape was exactly right. It was beautiful. I loved Echo Bend.

After my parents' ugly divorce, my mother must have needed an escape. She took charge and hauled my brother, sister, and me off to rural Hawaii to start a new life that ended up being far worse than the one we'd left behind. Fortunately, we were again living in a rural setting that allowed me to further cultivate my burgeoning escapism. Even indoors, alone, I'd sit on my bed and dream of finer things. I created in my imagination a sliding glass door to replace the small, confining window and, just beyond it, a relaxing deck that spread out several feet. At its edges were large pots with blooming shrubbery that shaded a soft, beckoning seating arrangement. I knew what I wanted; just because I couldn't have it didn't mean I wasn't going to dream about it.

From my childhood experiences, I was well aware of how cruel and devastating reality could be. The corporeal world was an ongoing killjoy that stifled my childish ideals.

Even when I was an adult and freed of the constraints of my upbringing, I continued to be hampered emotionally by the limitations of life. I wasn't aware of what was wrong, just that something was off kilter deep within my being. But there was one thing I was sure of: I loved the idea of growing things.

In May of 1984, Steve and I were renting a small house in Portland. Our firstborn had come into the world the previous October. I was itching to get my hands dirty. We trudged out to the backyard and, while little Daniel sat in his stroller and played with toys, I painstakingly dug out a section of lawn that showed hints of being a garden— perhaps—a few years prior by the previous tenants. I hoed the soil, then raked it up into raised, straight rows and made sure there was just enough room to walk between them. I planted corn, onions, and a few strawberry plants. And, of course, green beans, subconsciously hoping to mimic my grandmother's talent.

As it turns out, those green beans plants quickly became a magnet for a tiny black bug I'd later learn was an aphid. Before the beans were ready to pick, it became obvious that the aphids were winning the battle so I yanked the plants out of the ground and threw them in the garbage. Although aphids are tiny compared to the tropical bugs of Hawaii, I hated all bugs, a feeling that would soften with age.

Although in those first few years I had modest success with vegetable gardening, I realized that it was the most labor-intensive form of gardening there is. When vigilantly tended, the plants can produce many a satisfying meal. I have my grandparents' example to prove this. But the vegetable garden demands a lot from the gardener. She can't neglect it or things quickly get ugly.

Of course, any garden will entail a certain amount of labor, unless you have the means to hire your own landscape crew. It isn't the hard work that bothers me. It's that I like to have that hard work pay off. It seemed that, for me, the more I toiled, the sadder my veggie gardens always looked.

I think one of the perks of gardening is what we learn about ourselves in the process. We learn what our strengths and weaknesses are. We learn what makes us break out into a "happy dance" and what makes us clench our fists and cringe.

Through years of trial and error, blunders and blisters, I've learned that I require something more than a crop from the land I'm fortunate enough to call my own. I'm not satisfied with straight rows of corn or lettuce. I want an oasis. I want to feed my soul as well as my palate. I want the whole package.

I derive an incredible amount of pleasure from inhabiting my garden and partnering in its vigor and success. Still, it isn't always a joy ride. There are easily as many failures as there are successes. But they're all opportunities to learn.

Successful gardening, whether it is a summer vegetable garden or a year-round backyard oasis, requires attributes such as patience and keen observation, persistence, and even faith. Sometimes it feels like a lesson in futility as the ravages of nature undo our hard work and cause us to throw up our arms and stomp our feet and retreat indoors, grab a cup of coffee—or something stronger—and consider taking up knitting instead.

But once we come to our senses and realize that the challenges are not insurmountable, we forge a plan and get right back out there and dig in.

One of my favorite quotes comes from comedian and actor Bill Cosby. "In order to succeed, your desire for success should be greater than your fear of failure." This is as true in the garden as it is for the rest of our lives.

Success feels really good and is highly addictive. There is little else in life that is more rewarding than standing back and admiring a completed project, knowing that your hard work has paid off. That feeling of accomplishment is addictive and gardeners thrive on it. It's the desire for success that fuels our efforts.

Fear of failure will likely always be a part of who we are, but hopefully it's just a nagging voice in the back of our minds, only loud enough to keep us from getting too cocky.

The parallels between tending a garden and attending to life are obvious. Maybe it's because life began in a garden that there are so many similarities: How plants become beloved friends through the seasons. How we learn to intuit their needs and cry over them if they succumb to nature's vagaries. How we similarly have our growing time and our rest time, our sunny times and our times of torrential storms.

Through these pages, I hope you'll be able to see a little of yourself as we laugh and lament over the peculiarities of this sometimes frustrating but always delightful thing we call gardening.

Chapter One ~ Discoveries

Our yellow house on Thompson Street was a modest ranch with a big fenced backyard. Steve and I hauled our worldly possessions and growing family here on a cold January day in 1986. Although I was mere days away from giving birth to baby number two, I stole glances at the backyard with hopes of a future garden.

On the west edge of the lot was a towering big-leaf maple. Early on, I welcomed the majestic figure with its ability to offer a shady respite from summer's sunniest days. But I soon learned that this guy had the annoying habit of dropping his leaves consistently from July onward. With an expanse of weed-infested lawn that refused to stay green, my backyard tended toward savanna rather than the lush flower-filled oasis I fantasized about.

Those years, with a baby and a toddler to care for, my garden-making consisted mostly of gazing longingly outside while washing the dishes or thumbing through seed catalogs while at the same time feeding my daughter. It didn't help that any attempt at traipsing outdoors was met with the worst that Old Man Winter had to throw at me. The Pacific Northwest was having a series of brutal winters.

This particular winter was exceptionally frigid. The pipes in the garage froze and Portland's infamous East Wind persistently hammered on the northeastern portion of the fence until it collapsed in exhaustion. Fortunately, the eyesore posing as a telephone pole stayed upright despite my fear of it crashing on the house.

Spring eventually came and, once a stack of new boards sealed up the gaping hole in the fence, I built raised beds with the old ones. They would serve as the future home for the garden I had already created in my head. There were four individual beds, each a four-foot square, with just enough room to navigate between them. Rectangular beds would have been ideal, but I wasn't about to summon Steve and ask him to use a power saw. I was too impatient to wait for a weekend and besides, power tools scared me.

For lack of a better term, I dubbed my creation The Grid.

The Grid was ill-fated, glaring evidence of my gardening ignorance. I hadn't considered how difficult it would be to lean and reach to the center of a four-foot square to weed or pick flowers or spread compost.

I blissfully wheel barrowed dirt to fill in my raised beds and The Grid was ready to plant. Although my history with vegetable gardening was somewhat disappointing, I wasn't ready to give it up altogether. Figuring that maybe those dang aphids were an anomaly, I was willing to give green beans another try, so I relegated one of the beds to them and a few other edibles such as lettuce and radishes. The three remaining beds would play host to my new enchantment: flowers.

The idea of growing flowers took serious root when I visited a friend's garden. She lived just a block away. Our houses were part of a 1950s track housing subdivision with identical floor plans. Unlike mine, however, her house was beautifully decorated with houseplants and had a tropical feel without the brash colors. Each time I visited, I envisioned ways to incorporate her ideas into my four walls.

We had similar-sized backyards, too, but while mine was the savanna, hers was Eden. With gushing—and somewhat pathetic— admiration, it didn't take long for me to believe that her gardening habits were worth emulating. In fact, with my own lack of personal identity, I decided that I wanted to *be* her. She was much older. She was smart and pretty and she excelled at everything and, well, I sort of worshipped her.

It was her enchantment with hybrid tea roses that really got me thinking about flowers. I envied the luscious long-stemmed beauties that she was always sharing with people. To my admiring, idealistic eyes, she was pretty much perfect in every way, always giving and sharing from her vast cache of wisdom and resources. Without my own repository of either, I decided that growing flowers to share with people was something I *could* do.

Only much later would I learn how apropos the pejorative "black spot on a stick" is when referring to the overly-hybridized, long-stemmed rose. Being unwilling at this point to invest the money to purchase rose plants, I succumbed to Park Seed Company's alluring full color, flower-filled catalog and opted to go the route of the more-bang-for-your-buck flower seed.

The seeds successfully sprouted and grew and bloomed and before long I was giving away vasefuls of beauties just like my friend. My desire for pretty things grew as quickly as the plants. I expanded my horizons by learning the differences between the one-season or cold-sensitive *annual* that would die after a hard frost as opposed to the recurrent *perennial*. I loved the idea of growing plants that could survive the winter and emerge bigger and better the following spring. But, of course, the drawback to perennials was that their bloom-time was significantly shorter than it was for the annuals. That was the trade-off for their hardiness. Since I couldn't make up my mind which to grow, I grew both.

While roaming the perimeter of the backyard, I'd think about adding new flowers to the borders. The east side fared pretty well, with full sun and decent soil. The west side, however, was much too shady under the maple tree. The only thing that grew there was dust or mud, depending on the time of year. It was a perpetual challenge to my novice abilities, so I allowed my son to play here, digging holes and building forts.

One day I noticed a bit of green at the base of the maple tree that turned out to be a small plant tucked in a pocket of soil between the tree's serpentine roots. My first thought was weed! but I couldn't identify it as such. It was small, all right, but with a powerful fragrance when I touched its leaves—a spicy, almost bitter, pungency. As I stood and stared and marveled at the audacity this little curiosity had to pop up in the most inhospitable of places, I decided to dig it up and move it to a spot in one of my raised beds so it could gain a foothold and thrive and maybe even bloom. I was curious to see its flowers.

Looking back, I realize I was ignorantly playing with fire, honoring the "blessing" of an uninvited plant I'd later learn could either be termed as a volunteer or a thug, depending on the behavior of the thing. I suppose I could blame it on my grandmother's DNA. She had a penchant for plant foraging. I remember walking with her, my grandpa, and my siblings to Whistler's Bend Park just up the road from her house. She'd always bring home driftwood or a rock or some plant to use in her lavish garden.

It wasn't long before little white buttons emerged in lax clusters on a two-foot tall plant. They looked like tiny daisies with a double layer of pristine white petals and a soft, chartreuse center. I brought them indoors for bouquets that would last an entire week. If I left a few flowers on the plant, they would produce seed that would grow a new plant the following year. And, during a mild winter, the entire plant would stay green. Eventually I learned that I was growing the double form of Feverfew. Double meaning that the petals form a double layer, making a fuller flower. There is a single variety as well that has a bright yellow center. I learned that for centuries herbalists had used Feverfew to treat all sorts of ailments. Among them were headaches, stomach aches, tooth aches, and, no surprise, fevers!

Many years later, with several gardens under my belt, my current garden is filled, perhaps a bit too much, with the offspring from that very first mysterious emergence under the maple tree. Sometimes when I'm strolling down my garden paths and I see those sweet flowers blooming brightly, I remember back to that tiny forerunner so many years ago. It astounds me how easily I could have missed out on a special plant if had I ignored my curiosity and walked away or made the hasty assumption that the plant was a weed and tossed it in the wheelbarrow.

Life is made up of lots of little Feverfew plants—curiosities that start out as little more than a small nudge or inkling, a random occurrence that might not make sense and could be easily eschewed. Eventually, however, if we choose to keep an open mind, and even nurture it a bit, something interesting will develop. And with time and observation, we'll discover its significance in our lives.

As I glance at the Feverfew clumps stationed at various locations around my garden, I feel a sense of gratitude for the experience and the lesson that began when I noticed that first tuft of green under the maple tree.

Chapter Two ~ Bloom
Where You're Planted

During the majority of my early years, I lived with a severe anxiety disorder. It sucked. I didn't understand what it was, and for years, I was too afraid to seek help, which, of course, just perpetuated the problem. Now that I'm in treatment, I understand it better and don't blame myself for something I had no control over.

My anxiety originated, at least in part, from my traumatic birth. I was born breech in 1960 when doctors routinely used forceps for such deliveries. I must have fought like hell because I remember as a kid my mother telling me that when I was born, I was "all black and blue."

With the stage firmly set—ironically the doctor who delivered me was Dr. Stage—my anxiety increased dramatically by living with a raging, violent father. Without any practical help or parental nurturing, I was always frightened and on edge, but discovered solace in being outdoors, as far away as possible from the unpredictable grownups in my precarious life. This, along with the aforementioned DNA of my grandmother, might be the most viable explanation for why I love gardening today.

Fortunately, during at least a portion of my growing up years, my parents chose rural living. When things got too scary in the house, I was able to escape outdoors where I built forts and rode my bike and claimed the world as my own. However, it wasn't until I was twelve and living in rural Hawaii that I began to notice and fall in love with plants.

One of the first to win me over was the Plumeria. As I recall, the flowers grew on a rather gangly bush with foliage similar to the Rhododendron. It was easy to root and grow. And those intensely fragrant flowers were to die for. My mother was not a gardener and I don't recall where she got the plants for our yard. Maybe she stole them. But I remember breaking off the tips to start new plants in coffee cans with dirt from the yard.

My non-gardening mother was also not big on raising kids. She was more interested in appeasing my demanding father, which is understandable, although I don't recall him knocking her around like he did us kids.

After her divorce, she was more interested in finding a suitable replacement than looking after her traumatized, unruly brood. She was gone a lot. I used to picture her wowing the Michael Douglas-types while seated in high-class lounges along Hilo's Banyan Drive. She was a very beautiful woman, svelte and polished to perfection. I'm sure she turned many heads. I was hoping she'd bring Michael Douglas home because I harbored a secret crush on him as he saved the Streets of San Francisco from the thugs of society.

There were a few times when my mother, completely out of character, turned her attention towards my brother, sister, and me. It felt oddly pleasant, seeing her twirled hair from the backseat as she maneuvered the car around pot holes and tangled underbrush on Beach Road. As a pre-teen, I didn't think too much, just lived in the moments, as strange as they were.

Bumping and swerving along at a snail's pace, I looked out my window and spotted what I'd later learn was Lantana. It was a tall specimen with hundreds of yellow and pink flowers. I grabbed and pulled as many as I could and tried to determine whether its unique piquancy was pleasant or not. To this day, whenever I catch a whiff of Lantana, I'm immediately that kid again.

There were other botanical prizes to be found along Beach Road. Kukui trees were aplenty so we'd gather bags of mahogany Kukui nuts and try to make leis, but gave up since our mother was sensible enough not to leave us alone with a power drill. She *did* allow us to use a machete to remove the outer husk on our found coconuts, and, when I think about it now, I marvel at the fact that my siblings and I all survived with a full set of fingers.

I remember feeling like a real, living explorer as we wended our way along the farthest reaches of the Big Island. I don't remember if my mother spoke much. She smoked a lot, though. She always kept a couple of packs of cigarettes in her purse. They were either Parliament or Eve cigarettes with those pretty floral filters. There were a bunch of other womanly curiosities in her purse, too, and I wanted to dig in and explore it as much as I wanted to explore Beach Road.

There weren't that many outings, but on one in particular, my mother obeyed an impulse to turn into a nondescript, overgrown driveway. A few seconds later, the vegetation gave way to a sea of succulent, scarlet flowers with Pinocchio noses enveloped in deep green, heart-shaped foliage—an abandoned anthurium farm! As I remember it, a decrepit house was perched just on the opposite side of the driveway and tall shrubs and trees surrounded the entire area, enclosing us in a world of secrecy that easily rivaled Alice's Wonderland. Although I was delighted with our discovery, I was forced to deal with my anxiety by telling myself that *this* time, because my mother was with me, it was *okay* to trespass.

My sister, brother, and I picked as many flowers as our arms could hold and stuffed them into the trunk of the car. We traipsed around the waist-high undergrowth and picked tennis ball-sized limes from an overhanging tree. Then we summoned the nerve to walk over to the house. The doors were locked so we couldn't continue our exploration indoors. I felt a subtle sense of relief. It's one thing to trespass on someone's land, quite another to go inside their house.

As I recall, my mother facilitated one or two additional plant foraging expeditions. But once we returned home, she was aloof once more and left my sister, brother, and me to deal with our booty. I'm sure some of our plants died, but I don't remember them now. I remember everything thriving, despite the childish ignorance of the caretakers.

Among our plant treasures, were two small, dark green coniferous-like trees that grew near the beach. From my research, I think they were Ironwood Trees, but I can't be sure. We dug them up and planted one by the garage and one by the road and they both seemed happy with their new surroundings and grew quickly.

We found—stole—a cool looking Agave that started as a tiny rosette, but tripled in size seemingly overnight.

I remember planting papaya seeds and pineapple crowns and harvesting their fruit. We planted a coconut that grew into a tall tree. Somehow, we came by several Hibiscus shrubs and a split leaf philodendron. Both grew happily.

Despite these successes, the yard was still not much to look at. My mother, who, as I mentioned, was clearly *not* a gardener, opted to have the entire area top-dressed with black cinders. Likely she figured they would keep the weeds in check, the equivalent of bark dust here on the mainland. I suppose the cinders served their purpose to some extent. But it wasn't exactly a landscape that would elicit oohs and ahhs and visits from trendy and talented photographers.

My four-year stint in Hawaii was divided. Part of the time was spent dodging bullets either at home via an angry stepdad or at school where my sister, brother, and I were scorned racial minorities. The other part was spent outdoors. Looking back, I know without a doubt that the relatively carefree time spent in nature was my saving grace. Often after school or following a particularly violent run-in with my step dad, I'd take my wounded spirit and body and hobble outside and find my respite. The best of times followed the worst of times and rejuvenated me for the next worst time.

I think for many of us, being outdoors—either to garden, to hike or to just be—is a form of therapy. It connects us to the natural world. The quietness soothes our noisy souls. The fresh air cleanses us and the sunshine feeds us. And when the rest of our life is unpredictable and uncontrollable, tending a garden provides a way to use our hands and our bodies to *do something*. Sure, the problems will still be there when we hang up our garden gloves and scrape off our boots and come back inside. But our peace of mind will be much improved.

Three ~ Defining Myself

What do I like? What do I hate? What do I need? What makes me unique?

Better question: Who the hell am I?

People lucky enough to be raised under the tutelage of well-adjusted, nurturing adults can probably provide quick, succinct answers to these questions. Of course, it probably took some time and growing up to solidify these concepts. And no doubt there were challenges navigating through the maze of life's opportunities. Even those who grew up in a happy home have their unique issues.

Through my years of therapy I've learned that when kids grow up in healthy, nurturing homes, they're more able to discover their unique sense of identity. This is because as kids they're unencumbered by stressors and are free to create and play without the burden of fear and volatility from the adults in their care. The child-play they engage in helps connect them with their likes and dislikes and who they are as unique individuals.

On the other hand, kids who grow up in homes where safety is constantly in question have a more difficult time discovering their identity. Their concerns are divided. They're unable to devote themselves entirely to the play that helps define them.

I grew up without definition—anonymous, negligible, invisible. Episodes of *The Brady Bunch* were the extent of my parental nurturing. I remember Mike and Carol sitting down with one of their brooding offspring, Marcia, I believe it was. They gently encouraged her, easing the pain of a bad case of pimples—or was it a broken nose? At the time it didn't occur to me that Marcia had something I didn't. It's just how it was.

The ramifications of my upbringing meant entering adulthood with emotional handicaps. One of its cruel twists was the fact that I didn't even realize how troubled I was. Like navigating a darkened room full of furniture, each bump and bruise was a painful indicator to go in a different direction.

I floundered for a while in my ignorance then narrowed down my life choices to two. Already happily married—a miracle—I wanted to be defined as a *mother* and as a *gardener*. Later I would also include *writer*. Once that declaration took root, I found the realm of possibility exhilarating and freeing. I was married to a loving man. I could be a loving mother and a skilled gardener. I wasn't bound by my past. I was defined by my future and free to live it as I chose. Hooray!

Although my two older sisters were also gardeners, I didn't want to rely solely on their knowledge. After all, I was busy defining *myself* and my preferences.

I took advantage of two tangible ways of learning. The paramount method was empirical: the good ole fashioned trial and error, the get-in-and-get-'er-done approach. Working in the garden and observing what was and wasn't working made me happy despite the frustrations and sore muscles.

The secondary method was book knowledge. Being a visual learner, the mainstream seed catalogs became instrumental in helping me identify plants and learn Botanical Latin. In the days before the Internet, I spent many winter evenings poring over the glossy color photographs provided by Park, Burpee, and Thompson and Morgan.

When I was able to identify the most common plants, I began reading garden books. Margery Fish, Vita Sackville-West, Ann Lovejoy, Sharon Lovejoy were a few of my favorites. Many didn't have photos of the plants they were writing about, so in addition to my seed catalogs, I kept my *Sunset Western Garden Book* nearby. Although sparse where photos were concerned, it provided information that was good enough. I purchased my own copy after noticing staff at the local nursery referring to it. Even they didn't know everything.

Cultivating my identity involved embracing my gardening preferences — but I was still trying to figure out what they were. Although I was pretty sure it wasn't vegetable gardening, I'd commit several more blunders before I took garden design seriously.

I've still got my early garden journals. Every now and then I'll pull them off the shelf and chuckle over those scribbled seed orders of so long ago. I hesitate to get rid of those records for reasons I can't explain.

For a long time, I ignored anything purely green. Ultimately, it was the garden itself that nudged me towards a preferred color scheme, one in which green would become vitally important. From tall trees, medium-sized shrubs to what grew under my feet, green meant growth and health and vibrancy. Green would be the predominant color. Like the most urbane party host, green knows how to mix well and make all the other guests feel welcome.

I admit, I was—and remain—somewhat of a girly-girl. From the earliest of days, something about the color pink has made me smile. Be it the soft, subtle, barely-there blush to the deep, robust hues that the catalogs call ruby, it's all pink to me and all enthusiastically welcome in my garden. Also welcome are compatible colors such as purple, blue, chartreuse, and white. Warm colors are not necessarily banned from entry, but being mindful of color clashes, I think long and hard about where to place them.

Once I discovered the *It* factor of pink, decision making became easier. It's a lot like choosing toothpaste. With a plethora of choices staring you down at the grocery store, it can be dizzying. But once you know yourself well enough to understand preferences, you can just grab and go.

It astounds me how blessed we are in today's world. To have so many options at the ready is a concept that would have been inconceivable to our predecessors. Yet choices can also be a burden. Growing up I remember two when it came to toothpaste: Crest and Colgate. Because of the limitations, the decision was much easier to make.

The nursery is the same way. We used to have very few choices. Marigolds, petunias, and lobelia if we were lucky to find them. Now there are entire hoop houses devoted to summer annuals and entire acres devoted to shrubs and perennials, imported from the far reaches of the world like New Zealand and South Africa.

The concept of embracing choices and the freedom to take whichever road suits my fancy is a tremendous gift. Gardening is one of the ways I learned this. Walking through my garden, admiring the pink flowers of my Carpet Rose or my 'Elfin Pink' Penstemon or the walls and tufts of complementary green dancing in the breeze is one of the most rewarding ways I can observe my unique personhood. *And* it makes me feel good.

Chapter Four ~ It Takes All Kinds

There are as many different ways to garden as there are gardeners. The Minimum Gardener isn't too interested in the larger scheme of things. She's busy holding down the fort, involved in lots of indoor pursuits. She's a decent human being, but not much of a gardener.

Around the beginning of May, depending on the weather that year, she'll plant up a container or two with petunias and marigolds and set it by the front door. She'll faithfully water and fertilize and keep the plants happily blooming all summer and into the fall. With the inevitable killing frost, the container gets tossed out and there will be no activity until the following May, when blue skies lure Minimum Gardener outdoors again. She'll trudge over to Walmart or the local nursery, depending on her budget, buy a few baby petunias and marigolds, and repeat the cycle.

There is absolutely nothing wrong with this. Minimum Gardeners have other things to do and other ways to spend their money. I commend them for making an effort to beautify their porch with living plants.

My opinion, however, hasn't always been this magnanimous. When I began my serious affair with gardening, I loved marigolds and petunias but eventually I grew tired of *common* plants and sought out more exotic specimens, which, I have to confess, brought on a bit of an attitude. I was slightly *better*. And my superiority was easy to justify, given the audacity those Minimum Gardeners had to flaunt such lackluster horticulture preferences. Couldn't they at least stop partnering such clashing colors as hot pink and orange? I'd say to myself as I painted on a fake smile and rolled my eyes. I'm ashamed to admit that I harbored what my family refers to as a "bad-itude."

Somewhere along the line, I softened. I think part of it was getting older—and maybe medication.

The Minimum Gardener is the minimalist extreme; at the opposite end of the spectrum is the Die Hard Gardener. Toiling the soil is in the Die Hard Gardener's blood. He or she is a forward-thinker, avant-garde, innovative and highly developed, perhaps even ahead of his/her time. If a scientist took a microscope and looked at the Die Hard Gardener's DNA they'd see tiny things that look like leaves and shovels and garden gloves.

Die Hards have a stack of garden books on their nightstand. They subscribe to over two hundred garden blogs and don't have any money in the bank because they keep buying more plants, containers, and compost. If perchance Die Hard spots a dab of blue sky in January, s/he dons the work boots and heads out to tackle that bed they decided to make over the previous fall.

If TV producers were to bring back that game show, *To Tell the Truth*, from decades ago and the announcer asked, "Will the *real* Die Hard Gardener please stand up," I would jut upwards—probably doing so too quickly and getting dizzy. When I regained my questionable balance, I'd hold up my hands and show the audience the dirt under my fingernails to prove it.

For a few decades now I've been a Die Hard Gardener.

My husband Steve isn't in any way interested in gardening. Nada. Nil. Thankfully one of us is level-headed and makes sure we have a few dollars to buy groceries.

I'm lucky. My sisters are also Die Hard Gardeners. I don't see my oldest sister, Nancy, very often, but on my last visit a few years ago, I enjoyed seeing her towering cannas and sprawling pumpkins. We talked about our mutual love for flowers and bouquets and container gardens and seed-collecting.

I have more frequent contact with my sister Laura. Although we live on opposite sides of the state and rarely get to see each others' gardens, we can throw around Botanical Latin with the best of them and we get equally excited when our two favorite words—*plant* and *sale*—are used in the same sentence. We have fun reminiscing about our tomato plant anomaly years ago and the emotions surrounding our childhood haunts.

My friend Vicky and I have always shared a love of both gardening and shopping. When our kids were small, we'd leave our husbands in charge and mosey off to the nursery or thrift store to look for that something special for our gardens. And we always had a pretty good idea of what to get each other for our birthdays. I've got several of Vicky's gifts adorning my garden. They bring back pleasant memories.

I'm also blessed to be a part of a fabulous garden group. Ten of us meet monthly in various homes or restaurants to discuss relevant gardening topics like who has the most slugs eating their Hostas. Because we're busy with our respective lives, making the effort to meet on a regular basis keeps us connected. I always, always come away refreshed and filled with gratitude.

And if all of this weren't enough, I've got many online Die Hard Gardening friends, most of whom I've never met. It's a privilege and delight to visit their blogs where I can read about their garden happenings and see their amazing photos. There is some incredible talent in the blog world.

Die Hard Gardeners may still be only a small fringe of society, but we're here and we're united in our cause to cram as many plants as possible into our landscape.

Now when I see marigolds and petunias crammed into a pot sitting on a doorstep, I smile because they remind me of where I once was: a snooty, self-righteous plant snob. I've come a long way. There is no longer any temptation to roll my eyes and judge the purveyor. I'm all about celebrating the world's horticultural efforts, however minimal they may be. It's all good.

Ah, the principles of human nature. We start out green and hesitant of our abilities, fumbling around, trying to gain a foothold and make good on that vision that captivates us. With a little bit of success we quickly catapult to idealistic, fueled by a desire to establish standards that we feel everyone should abide by. We're young, impetuous, and we know everything.

As we age, we mellow and gain perspective. We appreciate peoples' differences because we're comfortable in our own skin and don't have anything to prove. We're honored to receive validation from those who believe in us, and we love the compliments we receive on our projects. But we'd be just as happy without them, spending our hours blissfully toiling away to the sound of birds and frogs, content with our efforts. We'd be so busy appreciating our surroundings that we wouldn't even notice the neighbor gal hauling her just-purchased petunias and marigolds to the porch.

Chapter Five ~ The Trial and Error Method to Self Awareness

I use the Die Hard Gardener label to describe people like me who are a little bit obsessed with all things gardening. It's meant as an endearing term—endearment mixed with wit, irony, a touch of sarcasm and maybe just a smidgen of woefulness.

The Die Hard Gardener can't resist having a constant, ongoing, year-round saga of garden happenings brewing on the back burner.

The way it works is a particular plant genus or garden design will capture the attention of the Die Hard. This is followed by the desire to learn, acquire, master, and wallow in the bliss of victory—or the agony of defeat—of that project. Oftentimes, before the first project is completed, the Die Hard will be captivated by another and another concept, flooded by ideas that require copious note-taking and a careful watch of the bank account by the Die Hard's hopefully sane partner.

I've thought about this through the years in an effort to explain—or excuse—the ebb and flow of my gardening passions. To be proficient at something, a person must have more than casual infatuation. One must possess an almost crazed enthusiasm, an unwavering fervor. They must have passion, gusto, eagerness. Apathy must be vanquished. Because they need to devote hours to learning and practice, they must develop an excitement for the task that eclipses most other things in life.

I liken Die Hard Gardeners to Olympic athletes. Everyone loves them. They're hailed as heroes. They're respected for their dedication, discipline, and determination. They work diligently because of their unwavering commitment to their cause. No one questions their mental stability as they eat, sleep, and breathe their obsession.

Eight hours of hard work each day is the minimum for not only competitive athletes but for doctors and astronauts and artists and novelists. And it is often the norm for Die Hard Gardeners.

My first obsession happened while tending The Grid, that area with four four-foot square raised beds built with old fence boards.

It was the latter part of the 1980s and dried flower arrangements and wreaths were all the rage. I found something exceedingly alluring about this media—authentic, once-living, perfectly preserved flowers, leaves, seedpods and stems. They made me swoon. The arrangements and wreaths I drooled over in the cute little decorator shops were quite pricey but they looked easy enough to make. Things always look easy before you try them.

I searched for affordable dried flowers but the only decent thing I could find were bunches of baby's breath for sale at the Saturday farmers' market in downtown Portland. Frustrated, I eventually realized how logical it would be to combine my love of gardening with my burgeoning desire for crafting. I'd grow my dried flowers. Seed catalogs made it easy with a section devoted specifically to plants useful for drying. I grew strawflowers of various sizes and colors, statice, baby's breath, and several less common flowers.

At the peak of perfection, I'd harvest my little beauties, bundle and hang them to dry in the dark garage. In fall, after the bulk of gardening was finished for the year, I'd bring my flowers in from the garage and spread them out in the dining room and embark on the crafting part. Good thing I had a decent vacuum cleaner because the entire process created a huge mess, with bits of crispy pieces littering the floor, the chairs and the table, not to mention all the spidery webs created by the hot glue gun.

At Christmas, I presented family members with their very own dried flower wreaths. I felt good seeing my creation hanging in their homes when I visited, even if it looked totally out of place and kept dropping little petals on the floor. I wonder if the recipients had brought it out only when they knew I was coming, then tossed it back in a closet once I left. I wanted them to love dried flowers as much as I did but it's entirely possible they didn't.

Having gained a blissful sense of expertise on all things dried floral, I entered my best wreath in the county fair. Second place was a mild disappointment but I could understand the judges' decision since the blue ribbon went to a sea shell wreath that was indeed spectacular.

I set up a display table at three different craft fairs. I did okay with sales but found it painful to watch people stare at my offerings then walk away and buy from a competitor several tables down. I was young, thin skinned, and took rejection quite personally.

When I finally came up for air and a clear-sighted reality check, I was forced to conclude that the whole endeavor was a tremendous amount of work with very little payoff. Why I needed to make such a big production out of it I cannot recall, but with the novelty gone I could see what a waste of time the whole thing had become.

Once my dried floral phase was dead and buried, naturally something else emerged to take its place. Roses caught my fancy, but not the hybrid teas that my friend was so good at growing. No, my affinity was for the miniature rose. I'd buy little healthy plants in various blossom colors. Some went in the ground with the idea that I could easily dig them up when we moved. Others went into pretty containers. The flowers were gorgeous, perfectly formed miniatures of the bigger ones my friend grew. The plants, however, were, to put it bluntly, awful. Blackspot and powdery mildew continually plagued the leaves and there was always a little pile of fallen foliage beneath the plants, exposing more and more unattractive stems. I didn't like using pungent fungicides; I was frightened by anything that originated in the indoor department of the plant nursery.

Eventually, the miniature rose obsession shifted onto some other pursuit that has also long since faded into obscure history.

New endeavors replace old, sometimes by the choices we make and sometimes through circumstances we have no control over. Our lives are fluid with comings and goings and ins and outs. As sure as there are taxes and death, there will be change.

As one phase morphs into the next, it leaves us a little more knowledgeable of the world around us. This might be the truest blessing of getting older. Having survived the trials and errors that can seem insurmountable in youth, we emerge knowing ourselves well enough to eschew the things that drain us of our energy and to pursue the things we are absolutely passionate about. We don't have to prove our worthiness by trying to fit our round selves into a square hole. We can say no. We have no axes to grind. We're here to leave our mark and it's a simple thing: to make the world a better place, one kind word and smile at a time.

Chapter Six ~ Ch-Ch-Ch-Changes: Spring's Optimism

When I was pregnant for the fourth and final time, Steve and I packed our kids and belongings and moved to the country. We'd been thinking about leaving Portland for quite some time and when friends were vacating their house in the country, we jumped on what we felt was a golden opportunity. By this time, I'd spent five years tending The Grid and raking up leaves from the ever-faithful big leaf maple. I countered any sadness over leaving by digging up and taking as many plants as I could. Several seedling Feverfews hitchhiked on other plants.

We were thrilled with the change of scenery and relief from the hustle-bustle of city life. The house sat on a hill surrounded by ten acres of towering Douglas Firs. A slope led down to a small lake. A clearing allowed just enough sunshine for a modest lawn and a few ornamental borders. At the onset I had a plethora of gardening ideas brewing. But mothering and an ominous turn of events that would—ultimately—lead me to my writing career put my garden-making on hold.

Eventually, although still in the throes of mental and emotional challenges, spring lured me outdoors for some Vitamin D therapy.

Any Die Hard Gardener knows that spring is when optimism is at its pinnacle and hopes for success cause us to do all sorts of things that normal people would find sort of … um … crazy. After all, we've spent the last five or six long months cooped up indoors with dog-eared plant catalogs and books by famous people like Vita Sackville-West and Dan Hinkley. Our brains are brimming with inspiration, and the need to *do something* is paramount on our minds.

As the kids played, I surveyed my surroundings and attempted to mentally resurrect my earlier ideas for the landscape. I knew I needed to keep things simple, yet I wanted to have it all, right now. How I wished I had the money to hire a crew and have them do the hard stuff. I could count on Steve to help if I asked him, but because I knew he didn't share my vision or verve, I felt it was unfair to ask him to do what I knew I was capable of doing myself. I could remember how as a kid I was forced into labor that felt like pure hell, all because I didn't understand the reasons for the work or the vision for the final result. There was no reward, no gratification. Even though Steve would be happy because I was happy, I didn't want to exploit his kindness. The visions were mine and the implementation would have to be, too.

I didn't have a lot to work with but hit the jackpot when I discovered a pile of discarded bricks hiding under a bramble of blackberry vines.

Once they were disentangled—and I'd gone through an entire box of Band-aids to keep from bleeding to death—I hauled them over to a clearing to build raised beds. Steve did put up a simple deer fence for me. I bought flower and vegetable seeds. I could envision swaths of blossoms and towering tomatoes thriving in my new garden. And that optimism fueled more inspiration. I even bought some raspberry and strawberry plants and cordoned off a spot specifically for them. I was thinking that with hard work and a lot of luck, I could have a garden that rivaled that of my grandparents decades ago. It was spring, the time for optimism and idealism.

***

The following year, I purchased several bare root roses on sale for two dollars each at a local variety store. At that point in my floundering gardening career, I was oblivious as to their poor quality or what Grade 1 or Grade 2 could possibly mean. I just eschewed the nagging doubts about their vigor and decided *what the hell?* If they died at least I wouldn't have wasted hundreds of dollars.

Oddly enough, a few of those roses flourished, defying their meager status. Before long, I was attaching exuberant yellow-flowering canes to Steve's deer fence. He laughed when I told him that this particular rose was named Golden Showers. Unaware of the connotation, I was disgusted when he explained it; I tried not to think about how he might have come upon that knowledge.

Most of my plants did okay in those brick-lined raised beds. However, there was one section that mystified me, a spot where nothing would grow. With my mind free to wander while pulling weeds in more fertile areas of the garden, I concocted all sorts of fantastical explanations. The ground was cursed. This spot was an invisible porthole to some malevolent netherworld and at night, if I were bold enough to venture out here, I would likely see blue smoke illuminated by moonlight rising from the ground in an obscure shape of something almost human. I was also having visions of blackberry vines coming to life and strangling me.

Finally, when I'd run out of weird ideas, I settled on the explanation that a previous owner must have poured something caustic on the soil.

***

My kids were as enchanted with our new digs as I was. The girls would bring me fistfuls of the wild daisies that grew along the edge of the gravel drive. They'd make mud pies and pick leaves and wildflowers for their meticulously crafted "dinners." My son was now a pre-teen and, thanks to the generosity and genius of his father, had access to the tools and was given a load of wood pallets to disassemble and reassemble into various building projects. He'd routinely wow us with his creations. He built a playhouse and tables and benches and, when Steve was home, the two of them worked on building a chicken coop.

At the end of the day, my kids were always dirty—a testament to their love of good old fashioned outdoor play. The Internet hadn't reached its tentacles into our household yet and the TV was closely monitored.

Although there were many gray days spent indoors during the five years we lived there, the ones I remember most are the blue-sky days, spent outdoors, breathing fresh air, while dappled sunlight nourished our souls. We drank up Nature's playground with birdsong echoing in the woods and a slight breeze dancing through the tree tops.

Looking back, I can see that although I was very troubled, I was equally enamored of my surroundings as my children were. Having parsed the great big world into a manageable size, we partnered with our Creator in designing little spots of loveliness. Whether it was a raised bed with frothy cosmos juxtaposing spiky coneflowers, or a playhouse wrought with nails and hammer, or a little pretend meal prepared on a home-built table, our simple joy was fueled by an intergenerational need to create and then sit back and admire our accomplishments. We felt empowered by our successes and this fueled our successive energies because as any gardener—or any kid—can tell you, it's never finished.

Especially in spring when anything is possible.

Chapter Seven ~ What Happens When You Don't Win the Lottery

In November of 1997, Steve and I packed up our four kids and moved once again, this time due to Steve's job transfer. After five years of living in a very rural setting, the idea of going back to a neighborhood seemed a little strange and scary, but I was happy with the house we were buying. It was twice the size of what we were leaving and with a big kitchen, two bathrooms and four bedrooms, it felt perfect for our up-and-coming teenagers. And a third of an acre seemed like more than enough space to create the garden of my dreams.

Again unwilling to part with my treasured plants, I scoured for whatever container I could find, including several five gallon buckets that formerly held laundry soap. I punched drainage holes in their bottoms and housed several freshly dug rose bushes, multiple clumps of Feverfew and other perennials, and even a half dozen of my raspberry plants. Thanks to our good friends John and Vicky, who owned a trailer, over thirty potted babies were safely transported to their new home. Once we arrived, the containers were unloaded and clustered under one of my Sweet Gum trees; that was where they spent their first winter.

The preeminent order of business landed squarely on Steve's capable shoulders: a fence to block the neighbor's house and keep their dog from pooping on what was a sorry excuse for a lawn. I'm afraid I was more than a tad impatient waiting for Steve to get the boards aligned and nailed but after several weekends of dedicated effort, it was finally finished and I had a fully enclosed backyard,

The area was a large rectangle, a hundred and thirty-five feet long and about forty feet wide. An aging pear tree was perched like a lonely island in the center. A healthy looking evergreen shrub that I learned was a Mexican Orange grew in one corner and two blatantly oversized Rhododendrons sprawled against the house. This was all I had to work with.

At least once in my life, it would be really nice to take possession of an established garden, I thought, surveying my surroundings and trying to ignore my freezing toes. The overgrown and saturated February lawn was not exactly hospitable to my flip flops.

How utterly delightful it would be to inherit a manicured lawn and healthy borders, brimming with an array of dazzling plants that were new to me. Where the former gardener had my vision and design style and where I could enjoy the fruits without the labor. No such luck, I thought as I gazed around at my blank slate. I knew all too well that life rarely plays by those rules. Enjoying a garden means work—or winning the lottery.

As I ambled around my new digs with a clipboard, paper, and pencil, I felt a sense of excitement over what would become of this space. The idea of persistent hard work didn't faze me because I kept the end result at the forefront. And I was young.

So, still trying to take no notice of my toes, I drew ideas on my paper: where my pathways would be located, where we would perch the playhouse my son built and the movers so skillfully disassembled and reassembled. Where would I plant the little vine maple saplings I'd spotted growing near the lake in full scorching sun? They begged to be dug up and brought here to live in dappled shade, so I listened and obeyed in honor of my grandma. And what about the rest of the booty anticipating their new homes while they waited it out under the Sweet Gum?

Spring arrived and I painstakingly dug out sod to create my garden beds—after Steve rented a sod cutter that took off a thin top layer that grew back overnight. I planted my roses and raspberries and perennials.

Eventually, the rain that Oregon is famous for went on summer hiatus and my plants grew big and bloomed. I was pleasantly surprised at how much faster everything grew here, in a mostly full-sun setting. What a contrast from the shady woods of my former garden.

Later that summer, I walked along my crispy, water-starved lawn, happy with my accomplishments and tolerant of my imperfections. As I gathered a small bouquet of Feverfew, I wondered if perhaps it was better that I was forced to toil the soil to create my own garden. Maybe taking over an established garden that the previous owner had designed would have left me dissatisfied on some level, like it wasn't really *mine*. Maybe I wouldn't appreciate it because I hadn't labored over it. Sure, it would have saved me several backaches but would I be as knowledgeable and savvy? Would I be aware that there are literally no rocks on this property and that the soil is mush in the winter? Would I know about the black plastic the previous owner misused as a weed barrier underneath the Mexican Orange? Being compelled to do my own work, mistakes and all, has forced me into an intimate relationship with my little piece of earth.

A lot can be learned by observing, no doubt about it. But a lot more can be learned by *doing*. Maybe winning the lottery isn't the best thing that could happen to a gardener after all.

Chapter Eight ~ Things That Make Me Want to Scream

When my kids were young, I had to share my garden space with them. Although it was the proper thing to do, deep down I think I resented it just a little. It wasn't the fact that their playhouse sat on prime growing real estate. I didn't mind that at all. In fact, I was happy to have a bit of whimsy situated in one corner. And I wasn't going to complain about the raised beds I handed over to them to grow their own plants, either. I wanted to create opportunities for my kids to enjoy nature and gardening and I knew the best way to do that was to make the garden theirs, too.

I taught them the virtues of ladybugs and the praying mantis. I helped them understand the needs of plants and why certain ones require more water or sunshine than others. I taught them the difference between an annual, a plant that completes its life cycle in a single growing season and is cold sensitive, and a perennial, a plant that goes dormant during the winter and would grace us with its presence again the following spring. I encouraged my kids to love flowers and devoted a sizeable area for ones they could pick to create bouquets or play food for their kitchen.

I read Sharon Lovejoy's ingenious *Sunflower Houses* and guided my little ones in creating a towering sunflower house of their own. We worked the heavy clay soil and buried sunflower and green bean seeds in a circle. We watched them grow and become a secret hideout seemingly overnight. I was a stellar mother. And I've got a bridge for sale.

It's true that I absolutely loved gardening with my young ones. They were as eager to learn as I was to teach and we were equally thrilled when a butterfly came to visit or we discovered a tree frog curled up in a Hosta leaf. We were all delighted by watching bumblebees buzz from flower to flower and monitoring the work of the mason bees as they filled their tubes.

But the moments I just described were just that: *moments*. The rest of the time my kids were:

- Kicking balls that hit and broke off a bunch of stems on my struggling fuchsia.
- "Cooking" in their playhouse and dragging all their play dishes around the yard and then abandoning them.
- Letting the wind carry their finished—and forgotten—artwork to the farthest reaches of the garden after hauling a ream or two of

paper out to the picnic table because it's more fun to draw outside.

- Leaving crumpled leaves and tattered flowers and mud pies on my otherwise pristine pathways, leaving their boots on the patio and socks in the playhouse, throwing rocks in the pond, and leaving their wagon, dolls, and blankets out in the rain.

I struggled. I wanted to scream. It was like someone was taking a paint brush, dipping it in black paint and swooshing it over my pretty canvas. I loved my children more than life itself but I resented their childish messes. And I hated myself for hating childish messes. I knew I needed to just relax, but I couldn't, despite the fact that in the back of my mind I was well aware that in a few years childish messes would just be a memory. My little darlings would grow up and be more interested in cell phones and trips to the mall than in nature and mud pies. I struggled to strike a balance between carefree nature play and keeping things tidy. I felt like a military mother, barking frustrated orders at cleanup time to reluctant, whiny kids. I battled discouragement. I knew a perfect garden was a futile dream, but something with just a *little* less disarray surely wasn't.

Also at play was my faltering self-esteem and its close cousin, peer pressure. I was reluctant to have people visit my garden because of its imperfections and the perceived judgment I would be exposing my vulnerable self to. Everyone I knew had a perfect garden—and perfect kids, too. What would they think when they stepped into my flawed estate? Surely they would never speak to me again, erasing me from their contact list, and labeling me as one of *those* people, whatever the hell that meant. It was a crazy, neurotic game I played with myself.

Eventually, true to form, my kids traded dolls and dishes for malls and My Space. But when they'd bring their friends over, they'd proudly show them the backyard. Then, later, let me know that their friends were impressed.

But there were still incidents that would make me want to scream. For example, witnessing the ravages of raccoons. They might be cute critters, with their little masked faces and fluffy tails, but they don't give a rat's ass about keeping people's gardens tidy. Rather, they seem to enjoy making a total mess of things because doing so just might amount to a single mouthful of food.

While my family snoozed peacefully, the regional raccoon population would decide a midnight swimming bash was in order. I'd stumble upon the mayhem the next morning and practically choke on my coffee. I never found any beer cans, but I was sure if I looked hard enough I'd find a bong and baggie in the bushes. The shredded water lily foliage was bad enough but when the main entrée was my beloved fish, I wanted to scream. I cried instead. I loved those fish.

I thought about getting a dog to keep the critters out of the garden but I was forced to table that idea when I witnessed Bowzer's destruction in the backyards of certain acquaintances. It seems a dog is as capable of wreaking as much—or more—havoc as a raccoon.

My garden cat was useless, of course. Smart but useless. Keenly aware that he was the vulnerable underdog, or should I say under*cat*, at the first harbinger of a coon convention he'd be at the screen door begging for entry. Of course, I wasn't aware that he was retreating to safety at this time of night because I was sleepwalking. It wouldn't be until I was fully cognizant the following morning that I'd be stifling a scream when rudely accosted by the evidence.

Through the years, I've mellowed. I don't think I'm quite the caliber of control freak I used to be. I try not to let negative run-ins with nature get me down, be it kids being kids, raccoons being raccoons, or wind being wind. It's all just part of the gardening package. Nature rarely complies with my desire for a perfect canvas, so, rather than getting all bent out of shape over a mishap, I try to just let life flow. Besides, I am aware that my backyard isn't strictly *my* canvas but that it's part of an entire dwelling.

Chapter Nine ~ Rocks and the People Who Brought Them

I have the best husband in the world. We met when I was seventeen and entering my senior year of high school. He was twenty-one and in college. I thought it was cool to be dating a college guy. He was older and smarter than those inane counterparts I was forced to spend six hours a day with. I was young.

That was in 1978. We've been together ever since. I attribute much of our camaraderie to something beyond conventional thinking, like a divine intervention that halted my downward spiral. Given my pathetically dysfunctional upbringing, I was sorely lacking in the life skills department. Picking a suitable life partner was about as foreign as a November without rain.

Steve has told me many times that it was my bubbly personality that attracted me to him. He liked my sense of humor and my happy-go-lucky attitude. I was a master at hiding my anxieties and fears and paranoia, at least most of the time. Even on the occasions when something bizarre leaked out, Steve seemed okay. I expected judgmental shunning and a swift right hook but Steve was a much gentler person than what I was used to.

Steve's dad wasn't a good provider, which forced his mother to be a penny-pincher. She was amazingly good at it, routinely going without so her children's needs could be met. She knew how to stretch a dollar from here to next Friday.

Steve didn't marry his mother. I was, and still am, a somewhat selfish person. Although I believe I'm a decent wife and mother, I am well aware of my own needs and I work just as hard to satisfy them as Steve's mother did to meet her children's. She made many sacrifices that I can't even fathom. I haven't needed to. I'm very lucky. I'm blessed.

After a few years of garden-creating in our newest backyard, I decided I needed rocks. Lots and lots of rocks. I wanted to use them to line my informal raised beds. I liked the look of verdant groundcovers spilling over rocky edging and small plants sitting slightly higher than the adjacent pathway. I was quite adamant about my need for rocks. Making them a reality in my garden was a bit daunting, though, especially when I began pricing them.

Checking out the cost of having rocks delivered was tantamount to a similar malady I suffered a few years earlier when Steve and I decided it was time to purchase a used Toyota minivan. It was a cloudy, cool day, as I remember it. With our brood bundled in their winter finery, Steve and I gazed with covetous affection at the body and interior of said minivan parked on some obscure used car lot on McLaughlin Boulevard in southeast Portland.

After hiking up a slipping bundle of joy so she'd rest on my more-than-adequately-padded hip bone, I allowed my innocent, unsuspecting eyes to rest on the bottom line of the lengthy label affixed to the minivan's rear window. Suddenly everything went black. Steve, quick on his feet, grabbed the baby, got her into her car seat and then turned towards me, lying limp on the hard, cold cement. After resuscitating me with ten minutes of CPR, he said to my weak, expressionless countenance, "Grace, honey, are you okay? Wake up."

Then he persisted to slap my cheeks several times. While in the background I heard the approaching sirens, he told me, "Grace. You're suffering from *sticker shock*."

Yep. That's how it happened. Okay, not really. It wasn't *that* dramatic but it was formidable in the sense that in a matter of seconds, I went from adulation at what I knew was a great idea to sheer and utter gut-wrenching disappointment. All thanks to that small thing we call money. The reality of the exorbitant monetary outlay involved in order to carry out my dream of a Toyota minivan was devastating.

Now, I might not be able to stretch a dollar like Steve's mother could, but I'd like to think I could hold on to it until, say, Monday at the latest. The idea of spending several hundred dollars on rocks just to please my gardening whim seemed excessively self-serving. Besides, we needed new towels. What kind of a mother was I if I had gorgeous rocks in my garden but my kids were drying off with holey towels?

Being the best husband in the world, Steve had *an idea*. I'd learned years earlier that when my brilliant, often quiet husband has an idea, I need to zip it and listen. He told me about an abandoned rock quarry just off the highway. He and my son had noticed it several weeks before while on the way home from a camping trip. People, who apparently had *my* idea, were loading rocks into their respective pickups.

I was skeptical, believing that when something costs nothing, that's about all that's going to come out of the deal: nothing. But I decided I'd feign excitement and gratitude and secretly hold my breath.

So my son, now a teenager, and my amazingly accommodating husband grabbed their heavy-duty work gloves and set off for the rock quarry to load as many rocks as they estimated were safe for the pickup—or until their backs gave out. Then they drove home. Knowing Steve, they probably stopped and ate lunch first.

As Steve backed the pickup into the driveway, I came out, all bubbly. I'd convinced myself that I was getting a pretty sweet deal.

And it was. The rocks were perfect. I hugged my menfolk and dismissed their generous offers to help unload them. Nope. I would gladly take it from here. I was completely undaunted, wheel-barrowing load after heavy load of rocks to corral my raised beds.

The only down side to this awesome arrangement was that the first delivery wasn't enough. This didn't seem to faze them, though. They drove back for more rocks and then back for more, five times in all.

I loved those rocks. I still do. When I look at them, I admire their permanence, their solidity, their intransience as, year after year, they flawlessly juxtapose the ever-evolving plants, mulches, and soils they keep in place.

When I reflect beyond the realms of gardening, I am so grateful for Steve and my son, so willing to gift me with such undeserved, sacrificial kindness.

I've never been very good at repaying people for their kindnesses. *Thank you* never seems adequate and anything I do in return seems dwarfed and insignificant when compared to the greatness of the gift I've received. I'm not good at reciprocating— or at least I feel as though I'm not. Perhaps it's a self-imposed blindness. Maybe giving opportunities are all around me but I'm blind to them. Perhaps it's too easy to talk myself out the perfect opportunity when it strikes. I'm pretty sure it's intertwined with the trait of self-doubt. It's one of the life skills I'm attempting to rectify all these years later.

Thankfully, I've got a great example of loving kindness in my sweet husband. The delivery of those rocks is just one of a multitude of examples. Granted, he desired compensation, but he's also very patient. I had a screaming backache by the end of the day.

Chapter Ten ~ Timing

As I write this, there are two containers of blooming hardy cyclamen just outside my courtyard window. Yesterday afternoon when I opened the door, I caught a whiff of their delicate fragrance. They're such pretty little things, shooting their slender necks up over the rim of the container, their tiny heads dancing slightly in the breeze.

They make me think of the friend who gave these to me many years ago. My youngest daughter was taking piano lessons. Judy was a no-nonsense, exceedingly talented teacher who also possessed an enormous heart. My daughter loved her. So did I. I saw her as a mother figure and I needed someone like her in my life. We forged a friendship from the very first lesson.

Judy and her husband Gene wanted help with their gardens so we arranged a bartering agreement where I worked a few hours a week to offset the piano lesson tuition. It was a win-win.

One of the areas needing my assistance was just outside the living room windows. It was a rather overgrown jumble of plants with no definition and it was bugging the heck out of Judy, a self-proclaimed neatnik.

"Get rid of everything," she declared as we surveyed the space. I could take home any plant that appealed to me and toss the rest.

I don't recall what else was growing there because I was busy trying to hide my elation over a spread of hardy cyclamen foliage next to the house. "What about this down here?" I asked nonchalantly.

"Yes, get rid of those weeds," she said.

While we walked around the area, I could hear my daughter practicing her scales on Judy's beloved Steinway just inside the house. Judy chatted, but my mind was on those cyclamen as I mentally devised the best way to move them without causing any disruption to their systems.

When the border was finished, Judy was pleased with the revisions I'd implemented. Not a gardener herself, she approved of my low maintenance concept as well as the deep cherry red blossoms of the now-famous Knock Out rose. We purchased two bushes and planted several similarly-colored hardy fuchsias to accompany them. The result was indeed gorgeous.

My daughter's piano-playing abilities astounded all of us. She was such a tiny child, but her dexterous fingers plucked a perfectly executed rendition of *Linus and Lucy*. I was one proud mama.

And I was thrilled with my booty. I planted at least a hundred little cyclamen bulbs in various spots around the garden. When I got tired of looking for available space, I started grabbing containers to house the rest. I gave some of them away, but the last two containers remain in my courtyard to this day.

What I most like about Hardy Cyclamen is the upside-down timing of their blooming. In the fall, when the rest of the garden is crying foul, they show off their pretty pale lavender faces.

The flowers and foliage emerge from round tubers that can get quite large as they age. While digging them up, I found a few that were roughly four inches in diameter, which told me they had been growing in Judy's garden for quite some time.

Once the sweet flowers fade, the little stems curl and coil, grasping a tiny seed pod. This is when the intricately patterned leaves emerge and grow into little heart-shaped wonders. They stay fresh and pretty throughout the winter and die off in June for a short dormant period before the flowers pop up again in August and September.

Ah, timing. It's September as I write this and most of my plants are showing signs of fatigue. An air of impending dormancy is palpable as I deadhead and clear away July's splendor. Just next to my pots of cyclamen is a clump of aging Solomon's Seal foliage threatening to drop its wayward stems on my little peepers.

In the plant world, timing is everything. Little DNA clocks dictate the behavior of each genus and species in nature. While I don't understand all the science, it absolutely fascinates me and I love observing how it all works. From my admittedly limited knowledge, I believe plant timing has much to do with the fluctuation of daylight hours. Each plant knows when to wake up in spring and grow and when to close down in fall and sleep.

Of course, there are those anomalies like the cyclamen that prefer to snooze during the summer months. Their fresh, spring-like flowers bloom in fall. How odd. How wonderful.

People have biological clocks, too. There is a predictable pattern to our physical happenings. We're born, we grow, we age, and we die. But our emotional cycles can be a lot like the cyclamen. We can bloom in the fall, when it's least expected. We can flourish with the cooler autumn days. We're fueled by the wisdom we've stockpiled for the impending winter of life. We can complement our surroundings, blooming where we're planted, shedding the light of our beauty on the dying world around us.

My little cyclamen, bobbing in the breeze, are a lot like me. I'm in the fall of my life, but I'm still going strong and hopefully beautifying my surroundings at a time when beauty might be in short supply. The cyclamen's growing cycle should give all of us hope. We're not late-bloomers. We're right on time.

Chapter Eleven ~ The School of Hard Knocks

The bulk of my gardening knowledge was obtained while attending The School of Hard Knocks. I know, I know, it's a pathetic cliché, but there is some universal truth to it, hackneyed as it is.

As a self-proclaimed, highly esteemed SHK alumnus, I like to stay close to my roots—Pun intended. I return often to receive additional merit badges to accompany the ones permanently inscribed on my arms and hands and ankles like hastily drawn tattoos. I like to call them my Continuing Education Credits.

Sometimes, when fellow alumni meet, we share our respective war stories, fully knowing we're in good company. We understand each other, and, given that our tales of woe are more like confessionals, we avail ourselves of all the compassion our classmates can provide. It's not about pride or bravery. It's a let-me-tell-you-how-stupid-I-was-yesterday relating, while lifting a pant leg to reveal a bandage covering an unlucky calf.

Being a klutz is just part of the SHK package. The school also doles out copious loads of humility. I'm thinking SHK's agenda is intended to both quell pride and kill impetuosity, but, since most attendees are a little stubborn, it can take literally decades to earn a degree.

At the time I enrolled, Bill Gates was still in his garage and the most futuristic image I could conjure up was Maxwell Smart's shoe phone. *Inter what?* Having the Google world at my fingertips was as unimaginable as a spring without slugs. But there were libraries, and it occurs to me now that perhaps before embarking on a new idea or method I should have taken a stroll down Dewey's Aisle 635 to research it first. But as a student at SHK, impetuosity rules. We grab trowel and gloves and *just do it*, blissfully undeterred by the possibility of failure.

I had sincere reasons for being such a good student in SHK, although I don't recall ever consciously thinking them through.

First, I was, and to some extent still am, a self-declared rogue. I didn't like the idea of people bossing me around, telling me to do things *their* way.

Second, I believed, and still believe, that gardening should be fun. It should be an enjoyable, calming exercise, a relaxing weekend departure from the rat race, an evening to decompress from the rigors of the office, an escape from the concrete jungle. Gardening should be free of rules and standards and pressures to conform. I don't want to spend my precious gardening time saddled with anxiety over doing everything perfectly.

Third, I'm lazy. Work is highly overrated. I'm in the garden to *create*, not to work. I'm finely tuning paradise, one pruner-snip at a time. Work is something else altogether and can wait for a rainy day. They call it house*work* for a reason.

One time, years ago, I saw a Famous TV Personality illustrating the *proper* way to seed a lawn. I found all of the rules and civility off-putting and I was daunted by the person's adamant step-by-step approach. I remember the host using a heavy roller to flatten the freshly seeded soil and then spreading crispy straw over the entire area. *What? Who cares if it serves to hold in the moisture? It looks ugly and the wind will blow it from here to the next county. I won't do it.* Years later, I still don't own one of those heavy roller thingies and don't know a gardener who does.

One of my earliest episodes of foolhardiness occurred when I was a freshman and still gardening in The Grid. I asked Steve to rototill a section of lawn so I could create an additional flower bed. I wanted to plant the Daisy and Lupine clumps I'd dug up during one of our drives in the country.

It has always amazed me how willing Steve is to suffer for the sake of my garden. He rented a rototiller and churned the grass under and back up again, around and around. Once his countenance held a not-so friendly-look of "My back hurts and I need a beer," I deemed the bed sufficiently pulverized. Steve then spent a few frustrating hours disentangling grass and muddy roots from the rototiller's blades before returning it to the rental place.

While he was gone and the children napped, I spent too much time doing something that felt strangely close to work, sifting and tossing large, insufficiently pulverized lawn clumps into a growing heap off to the side of my new bed.

Eventually, I blissfully planted all my weeds—er, *wildflowers*. Oregon stayed true to form and graced us with three more months of rain.

When I finally got back to my project-in-progress, I noticed grass blades shooting up throughout my new flower bed. Granted, the wildflowers were growing, too, which I suppose should have been a source of encouragement, but every gardener knows how easily weeds grow, especially when we're kind to them. Dang those tenacious grasses! No matter how mean I was to them, the moment I turned my back, they'd stick out their tongue, give me the finger, and snicker unmentionable things. Then, fueled by nitrogen-rich soil, they'd flourish, spoiling my becoming-pathetic flower bed.

I don't remember how I resolved this annoying situation. I think we moved. But I received special commendation for this feat—an especially humiliating Knock, which translated into a valuable lesson, simple, yet profound: *Before you rototill the grass, make sure it's quite dead first.*

Along with the plethora of klutzy merit badges permanently inscribed on various parts of my body, I've got a mental trophy case full of humiliating Hard Knocks. It's all very demeaning, because, deep down, I'm aware that much of what I take on would go a lot smoother if I would do my research first. But then I console myself with the thought that it's not necessarily *how* I've learned that matters, but the fact that I have indeed learned. And, besides, all the book learning in the world will never substitute for actually getting in there and doing it. So off I go to yet another adventure in gardening.

And it's while *doing* that a bevy of little—or not so little— hiccups along the way present themselves. These are the Hard Knocks, the lessons to be learned in the process of achievement and mastery.

And if we're listening we'll not just learn about gardening or some other worthy endeavor, we'll learn about ourselves too. If the knocks hurt so badly that we throw up our hands and mumble "to hell with it," we'll know that it's time to move on to other things.

However, if the knocks are minimal and we feel that familiar addictive sense of accomplishment we'll know that this endeavor, despite initial setbacks, is for us. Either way, the knocks are there to teach us.

Chapter Twelve ~ Ways in Which We Make More Work for Ourselves

From vast caches of experience, I state that if you're a gardener, procrastination is *not* your friend. Like a sweet poison, it might be smooth going down as you laze on a lawn chair and gaze at the clouds. However, when that gaze comes back to earth and rests upon what was once an orderly oasis, a nasty tummy ache will ensue. How do I know this? I learned it while attending the School of Hard Knocks, of course.

Procrastination or avoidance can ruin a garden. Fast-growing shrubs, trees and vines must be pruned at least once *every single* year, or they'll quickly get out of hand. I've got a lot of fast-growing shrubs, trees and vines in my garden. One reason for this is that I live in western Oregon with a mild—USDA Zone 8b—climate and fertile soil. Plants really love this part of the world and waste no time in making themselves at home.

The other reason for my fast-growers was due to my initial impatience. When Steve and I brought the troops to live here, I wanted a full-grown garden, stat. But, as we weren't lottery winners, I had to buy smaller, inexpensive plants, and wait for them to fill in. Patience not being my greatest strength, I compromised and bought *quick* filler-inners.

The upside was that they fill in quickly, making the impatient gardener happy about what she's created. The downside is that they fill in quickly, then keep on filling in, *way* past their intended height and girth. If unattended for any length of time, dealing with the results is a huge chore.

Take, for instance, my English Laurel plants. I chose them because they grow fast and I figured gazing at lush green plants was slightly more appropriate than staring straight into my neighbor's upstairs bedrooms every time I set foot in my dining room.

Those Laurels have more than achieved their initial purpose. They block the neighbor's windows, all right. And everything due east. We never get to see the sun or moon rise from our backyard.

Laurels are great plants and serve their purpose well. Some years, I sit on my lawn chair with my avoidance elixir and watch them reach towards the sky and think, They're sure lush. You gotta love a happy plant. But when I go near for a close up inspection, I'm daunted by the size of their trunks and their multiple arms reaching outward in every direction. Actually I'm more than daunted. I'm a little frightened by the untamable monster I've created.

The pear tree isn't quite so bad. By that, I mean its growth is moderate compared to the laurels. But, the annual task of removing the bazillion vertical suckers is a major nuisance. Due to my incessant whining, Steve always assists me in this painstaking endeavor. And while I'm hauling poky branches to the yard debris can, I'm silently congratulating my neighbors who had it right when they cut their pear tree down several years ago.

Last spring, after an entire decade of dealing with the annoying pear tree chore, I got a really bright idea. With my fear of power tools diminishing, I splurged and bought one of those electric mini chainsaws on a long pole. Work smarter, not harder would be my new motto, I decided. Yes, siree.

However, for reasons I can't recall—very good ones, I'm sure—the pear tree task never did get done. Even with a brand spanking new power tool for enticement, other tasks shoved pear tree trimming off of the honey-do list entirely. Or maybe Steve purposely put it off because he figured it would be more fun if it required twice the effort.

The results of procrastination are similar in all aspects of life, as I learned the hard way several years ago.

Apparently the parking meter was exceptionally hungry that day because, despite unloading my wallet, I still didn't feed it enough coins. I discovered this while hauling my fifty pounds of books out of the library towards the car and catching sight of my punishment in the form of a humble slip of paper on my windshield: a ten dollar parking ticket. I decided to ignore it because I knew that if I did, it would go away quietly.

A month went by and then, in the mail I was greeted with a very official looking past-due slip with a whopping five dollar late-fee tacked on. I quickly paid the bill in full and determined that throwing an extra quarter in the meter in the future was a prudent investment.

The lesson: Procrastination never pays, especially in matters of money—and weeds. Ignoring things doesn't make them go away. Sometimes, it makes them bigger, as evidenced by my pear tree.

One typical spring Saturday several years ago, the more I looked around my garden, the more my mental to-do list grew, including the eradication of a cluster of dandelion puffs I spotted growing in the raspberry patch. I was well aware that if I didn't get to them soon, a gust of wind would dislodge and render airborne an uncountable number of little fertile parachutes. A relatively small number of dandelions would quickly become a monstrous monoculture.

I had every intention of tackling the dandelions but, when I wasn't paying attention, Procrastination redirected me to the painstaking and time-wasting process of removing a boatload of tiny, shriveled Sedum leaves and other detritus littering the pebble topdressing on a pretty succulent container I left sitting out during a wind storm the previous week.

I'm pretty sure Procrastination is in cahoots with my genetic—blame the family—malady I like to call Busy Brain, or, more pseudo-scientifically, COS: Creativity Overdrive Syndrome. It happens most often when I'm presented with a multitude of tasks with a deplorably finite number of hours to complete them. On this day, my COS was in full-on mode, because before I was able to achieve pebble perfection, I was enticed by the hint of a sweet, lemony fragrance wafting on the wind straight into my nostrils. "Daphne," I said aloud, mimicking Barnabas and thinking I needed to check Netflix to see if I could watch the old *Dark Shadows* episodes tonight when my body was in too much pain to move after a full day of gardening.

Another whiff of Daphne's deliciousness reminded me that this shrub's early blooming flowers would be fading soon and I really should cut a few sprigs to put on my nightstand to perfume my bedroom and sweeten my dreams.

While offering up a silent prayer of gratitude, I stood upright, took another sweet breath, did a quick stretch to ease the cramp in my back, and grabbed the clippers. I found three nice little sprigs and walked back towards the house. I had every intention of going indoors to fetch a small vase for my sweet lovelies, but then my cat came trouncing up to me. I set the flowers down and bent down to pet Willow-the-Garden-Cat who was clearly a bit miffed by the empty spot in her dish. "Oh, brother, you cats are so spoiled," I told her, reaching over and rearranging what was clearly enough food. She seemed satisfied and began munching contentedly.

Rising too quickly made me dizzy, which made me forget what I was doing. Oh well. Oh, yes, the hanging basket of Bacopa that, thanks to the mild winter, was still alive but looking mighty thirsty. I scanned the deck for my watering can to no avail so figured it must be over by the faucet. Walking towards it, I noticed that the honeysuckle vine I was allowing to twine itself on the deck railing had already broken dormancy and was sending new shoots towards the containers sitting next to it on the deck.

"This is not good," I said out loud in a tone that implied the situation was tantamount to global warming. What if those vines decided to root themselves atop the soil in the containers, or worse—and more likely— completely smother the plants I had growing there?

Heaving a heavy sigh, I went in search of my clippers. Oh, yeah, right by the Daphne sprigs. *Crap, I've got to get those flowers into some water before they wilt.*

Another sigh, this time more determined. I walked back towards the honeysuckle and noticed the thirsty Bacopa. "I can't let you survive all winter and then die of dehydration in spring," I told it before walking, fully focused now, towards the faucet. I set the clippers down and filled the watering can. When it was full, I carried it towards the Bacopa, but noticed a huge slug crawling across the deck. Worried that I might step on him—wearing my flip flops—I set the watering can down and walked over to the shelf where I keep my garden gloves.

Tossing the little interloper into one of my weed buckets so he could enjoy a pleasurable last meal, I promised myself I would dump him in the yard debris can before he could slither back out onto the deck.

Now, what was I doing? Oh, yes, the Daphne blossoms. I brought them inside, found a small vase and noticed I'd left my laptop running. A half hour later—damn Facebook—I went back outside and noticed my poor Bacopa. I watered it and apologized.

Dictated by Busy Brain, several more projects came and went, getting the better of me that day. And while I was otherwise engaged, I neglected to tackle the dandelions, which quickly went from sunny yellow flowers to fecund seed puffs. In a matter of days, a dandelion plantation was born, forcing me to allot much more time and effort to my weed-pulling agenda—something that definitely resembled *work*.

I'm learning that knowing the difference between authentic planning and avoidance/procrastination can make a huge difference—in both gardening and life.

Sometimes, being lazy and procrastinating or being busy and distracted is okay. I really like bouncing from one job to the next, being sidetracked by a pretty flower growing by the fence or a flock of geese squawking overhead. And it's true that if I deal with certain chores on a regular basis, it makes life easier, but if I don't get to them, that's all the more reason to get out to the garden the next time.

My neighbors removed their pear tree. Most of the time, I really enjoy mine. Each situation, and each person, is unique.

Chapter Thirteen ~ The Lighter Side

So much seriousness. The world is full of stern people and pundits, experts who tout their various agendas, so sober and unsmiling — and all critical, of course. "You must do this. You can't forget to do that." They gesticulate with their own brand of sincerity. They require respect long before they've earned it.

The gardening world seems no different. Maybe the experts are not wearing designer suits and matching shoes, but the demeanor appears to be similar. At least, that was how I perceived it during the early years of my read-everything-garden-related phase. There were certainly a lot of firmly entrenched opinions, and they were written by the most staid advice-givers. Often, the guidance was relevant and appreciated, but the delivery was so serious, it made me think I was studying for a Master's degree in nuclear physics or something equally difficult. The message between the lines seemed to be that if I knew what was good for me, I would not dare take any of the instructions contained therein lightly or deviate from the imperative.

Granted, the world is a serious place and there are turbulent matters to attend to. But at the end of the day, or maybe a few hours before, I believe we should all be able to relax.

By learning to lighten up, to laugh and relish the humor that is there for the taking, the world becomes a softer place. Not, obviously, humor at the expense of others. Cruel humor isn't funny. It's just mean. But laughing at our own blunders, especially when they deal with our hobbies, why not?

I remember when and how I learned to not be quite so serious where garden-learning is concerned. It was a serendipitous moment because I can't claim to be a regular viewer of *Regis and Kathy Lee* or whatever it's called now. But the show was on TV that fateful day and the guest was a rather flamboyant, middle-aged woman discussing plants to a rather indifferent, somewhat temperamental Regis Philbin. Initially, it was the plants that caught my eye, a row of luscious green beauties lined up on a table. The woman was espousing the virtues of each with a dramatic flair that, to my knowledge, was unheard of in the community of garden "experts." At least the ones I had sat under.

At the end of the segment, Mr. Philbin referred to his guest as Mrs. Greenthumbs, a.k.a. Cassandra Danz. I liked her. She had spunk. She was unpretentious yet confident and she knew her stuff. And she'd written a book.

I was quick to get on the phone to the bookstore. I couldn't remember the title of the book so I just uttered a hopeful "Mrs. Greenthumbs?" to the clerk on the other end of the line, figuring she'd already received at least a dozen such calls from other customers who had been glued to their TV that morning.

A few weeks later, after receiving a call from the bookstore, I hightailed it over to the mall to nab my copy of *Mrs. Greenthumbs: How I Turned a Boring Yard into a Glorious Garden and How You Can, Too* by Cassandra Danz.

And that book was how I learned that gardening and humor can successfully coexist. Gardening doesn't need to be a stuffy, hoity-toity endeavor. Not according to our beloved, now departed, Mrs. Greenthumbs. And not according to me either.

Ms. Danz's book takes the reader through a year, month by month, as she and hubby Walter transform their backyard wasteland into a beautiful garden. Hardly a boring undertaking, we're invited to laugh right along with her as she entertains us with garden wisdom and lots of humorous digressions.

The book begins with a lament over the forest of pesky Ailanthus trees growing in the derelict yard of the Danz's newly purchased home in Hudson, New York. "It's a tree that could grow on Mars. One tree can put out thousands of seeds... It is the rodent of the arboreal world and when you cut it down, twenty more will sprout from the roots, like unwanted facial hair."

My favorite anecdote occurs in the month of July when the happy couple stops at a garage sale at the home of "the local dysfunctional family." While Walter waits in the car, Mrs. Greenthumbs steps out and looks at the offerings. Broken motorcycle parts, a helmet with a bullet hole, a do-it-yourself tattoo kit, old gun racks, several striped shirts with numbers on the back, a box of forty-five caliber bullets, essentially the kinds of things Bonnie and Clyde might sell. But nothing says "buy me" quite like the healthy clump of Artemesia growing under a dead Yew.

Dauntless in the pursuit of plant material for her garden, Mrs. Greenthumbs grabs a dollar bill from her purse, musters the nerve to walk over to the man with "Stud" tattooed across his knuckles and sheepishly asks, "C-could I buy a small clump of that gray plant over there?"

Stud's reply is a blearily mumbled, "Whah, whah the fuh?"

Once he's had time to let Mrs. Greenthumbs' request sink in, he saunters over to the clump in question, grabs a fistful and yanks, then hands it to Mrs. Greenthumbs who is all too quick to get back to the car before, well, who knows what?

And the ensuing prose highlights Mrs. Greenthumbs' introduction to the thugs of the plant world and her need to impose a "pushy-plant law."

I've never grown the particular species of Artemesia Mrs. Greenthumbs coveted that summer day, but I have had experience with thuggish plants, the ones that seem hell-bent on taking over the entire garden.

Her story reminded me of a time when plant lust fueled my shameless, brazen begging. At that point in my gardening career, I was already well-versed in the curse of the plant thug; however, groveling for plants has never been out of the question.

There was a house I routinely passed on the way to town. At the edge of its front yard were two easily six-foot tall *Rosa mutabilis* bushes that would bloom like mad from May to October. The single blooms open in a soft peachy color and gradually morph through several stages as they age, ultimately finishing in a gorgeous deep pink. From my car, the effect of multiple blooms at various stages and colors was magical.

Overlooking the fact that I had no room for such a large beauty in my garden, I decided that I *needed* to have my very own Mutabilis rose bush. I called around to various nurseries but none had it in stock. Apparently, at the time, this was a rare rose. Fueled by my shameless unrelenting plant lust and likely the principle of wanting something all the more because I couldn't get it, I grabbed my garden buddy Carol for support, pulled a five-dollar bill out of my wallet, and collected my clippers. Quickly, before I lost my nerve, the two of us drove up to the house where the rose of my dreams was growing.

Channeling Mrs. Greenthumbs for support, I sheepishly smiled and addressed the nice woman who answered the door, waving my five-dollar bill around in an effort to be persuasive and banish any air of rudeness.

"Um, hi. I live up on the hill over in that direction," I told her, pointing, so she would clearly see that I was a neighbor and not a serial killer. "Your Mutabilis roses are absolutely outstanding. I'd like to know if it would be possible to buy a few cuttings." And I shoved the money at her.

Unlike Stud, she refused the money and told me to have at it. And only after downplaying her efforts at caring for them, which was completely untrue, of course, but revealed her humility which I thought was nice.

While Carol watched—either impressed or mortified, I'm not sure which—I snipped off five tips. At home, I prepped them and then placed the little darlings in soil and waited for them to grow. One of the five survived and is well over six feet tall at the peak of summer. It has joined the gang in the garden, elbowing its neighbors for space.

***

Mrs. Danz went on to write a second equally entertaining and insightful garden book titled *Mrs. Greenthumbs Plows Ahead: Five Steps to the Drop-Dead Gorgeous Garden of Your Dreams*. She was also a contributor to the now-defunct *Country Living Gardener* magazine. I cut out and saved all of her columns.

Since becoming familiar with Casandra Danz's work, I've found several equally entertaining and insightful gardening experts. But I am forever grateful to Ms. Danz, who succumbed to cancer in 2002, for making the introduction.

Chapter Fourteen ~ Imperfections? What Imperfections?

Gardening is not for the faint of heart. It is a pursuit that brings you face to face with your foibles and inadequacies. But Die Hard Gardeners seem to be gluttons for punishment. Our blunders are routinely exposed and trampled upon, but for some mysterious reason we face them head-on—and sometimes even laugh. After all, most of them are not catastrophic and can be filed in the *I should have known better* or even the *Okay, not a big deal* category.

Case in point, I have this Loropetalum, a gorgeous, burgundy-leaved arching shrub. Its common name is Fringe Flower and it is a distant relative of the witch hazel, which becomes obvious when Loropetalum is in bloom. It produces similar froths of linear-shaped petals, only instead of the yellow or russet that witch hazels produce, Loropetalum's blossoms come in the richest pink. And partnered with the burgundy foliage, the effect is nothing short of stunning, especially for a lover of pink flowers such as I.

My problem is that, well, I need to know what I'm growing. Gardeners like me crave information. We're not satisfied with only common names. We want facts, like the genus and species and the cultivar names. We're just wired that way. Knowing both the genus and species of our plants is like knowing the first and last name of our acquaintances. The genus is the last name: more general. The species is the first name: more specific. I don't think this is a coincidence.

Some plants, like petunias and marigolds, for instance, are common enough that for most of us more particulars aren't necessary. These plants are the equivalent of, say, the furniture store called Smith's or Johnson's. The last name and address are all we really need.

On the other hand, for a prospective life-partner, we want to know a few more details. The first and last name, of course, but also who the relatives are and whether or not any of them have seriously nefarious pasts.

Particulars are really important. We want the specifics, the attributes and the liabilities. The more we know about a plant, the better.

Die Hard Gardeners are never satisfied with knowing only what I call the nickname of the plant. Fringe Flower, the nickname for Loropetalum, while nice, doesn't say much, other than that the flowers are fringy. And Mrs. Greenthumbs' encounter with Stud? I'd venture to guess this was just his nickname. In the plant world, we don't say nickname, though. We say common name.

Sometimes common names can confuse us because they're attributed to more than one plant. Hmm…which Stud do I want?

For instance, False Indigo. A Google search will bring up *Amorpha fruticosa, Amorpha nana, Baptisia australis,* Bastard Indigo and River Locust. If I know Stud's first and last name, I'll know that I'm looking for George Clooney and not Mr. Garage Sale.

My quandary with my Loropetalum is that, although I know the genus and species of my lovely, I don't know the cultivar. Thanks to a crippling case of plant lust, I needed to have not one but three different cultivars of Loropetalum, two of which did not survive. Because of my sporadic note-taking, I didn't document the details of the deceased. I'll probably never know which cultivar I'm growing. It would be nice to know.

In a perfect world, I wouldn't be so neglectful. Knowing myself, however, I'll probably make the same mistake in the future because I'm not terribly motivated to change this behavior. There are more pressing things that need improving and I'm choosing my battles.

Sometimes we just have to shrug it off and embrace our imperfections. It's very freeing.

Chapter Fifteen ~ Dear Santa

December. The garden has gone to sleep but the gardener is awake. There are nagging chores. I can see them when I look out my dining room window. Leaves from the Japanese maple litter the patio and pond, and arching brown spears that were just a few months ago a pretty clump of Japanese Forest Grass demand a haircut.

I'm ignoring all those demands right now because the weather is inhospitable and there are indoor matters of higher importance.

December is the *giving* time of year. It's the time when we open our hearts and our wallets and think of those less fortunate, consider how we can help make the world a better place, and reflect on ways in which we can become better people, enhancing the quality of life for ourselves, our loved ones, and others. We selflessly give and feel warm and fuzzy for doing so.

But December is also the time to think about *getting*. Oh, sure, we're making a list and checking it twice, but when we go shopping, there's always a slight deviance from that list when we see a thing or two that has our name written on it. We just ever so stealthily slip it into our cart and continue perusing the aisles for everyone else.

In the garden, as in life, regardless of our gratitude for all the ways in which we've been blessed, there are always at least a few things that we don't have but wish we did. We may not admit our wants to anyone because they seem kind of outlandish and maybe even impossible. Plus we don't want to appear ungrateful.

Me? I don't mind appearing ungrateful at all. I've got me a *wish list* for Santa.

The garden wish list project does not originate with me, however. The honor goes to my online blogger friend Christine. She lives in Alaska and if anyone deserves to implore Santa for gardening assistance, it's someone who gardens in Alaska.

Last year, always pragmatic Christine wrote to Santa and asked for more efficient moose and bear patrol for her garden. Moose and bear are not a gardener's friend. They like the same plants as gardeners and show their affection by eating them down to stubs. And if that's not bad enough, they don't possess the wherewithal to clean up after themselves. I think Christine's request was perfectly justified.

Christine also wisely requested a hybrid tomato that would ripen in her short growing season of, say, four weeks. It certainly can't hurt to ask.

Because I toil the soil in western Oregon's comparatively balmy USDA Hardiness Zone 8b where winter temperatures rarely drop below twenty degrees Fahrenheit, my needs —read idiosyncrasies—are slightly different than Christine's.

My humble letter to Santa:

Dear Santa,

I've been good. All year. Mostly. I've whittled my list down to five simple requests because I know you're busy.

I would love it if you could replace the three, seventy-five foot tall Sweet Gum trees in my front yard with something that grows fast, so it will hurry up and shade the house next summer, but will drop its leaves in, say, three weeks instead of three months to shorten my cleanup time. If this is outside your budget, dear Santa, I'd be grateful for a perpetual, gentle but effective wind to send all of the fallen detritus into the neighbors' yards or, better yet, down the hill into oblivion.

On the subject of replacements, I'd love it if you would be so kind as to replace my now-in-its-fifties body with that of perhaps a healthy eighteen-year-old. One who can bustle through garden chores with young, limber muscles, free of the weight of age. One caveat, though, if I may. Pretty please, only from the neck down. I would like to keep my body from the neck up because I really need to hold on to my current brain, flawed though it may be. I don't want to have to re-enroll in the School of Hard Knocks, because twice in one lifetime might actually be worse than gardening with a middle-aged lower body. Thanks Santa. You're awesome.

And, Dearest Santa, I would love just an ever so slight expansion of the backyard boundaries. Specifically, could you move the fence just a wee bit to the east so I can have a tad more room for pruning the laurel bushes and planting all the ornamental grasses, lavenders, and drought tolerant shrubs I won't be able to resist in the coming year? I'm sure the neighbors won't mind. In fact if you do your magic while they're asleep, I bet they won't even notice.

And on the subject of zones, Dear Santa, could you please change my Zone 8b garden to a solid 9 so the winter temperatures would remain warm enough to keep alive all of those frost-sensitive plants that begged me for a home last summer? I think if those plants didn't succumb to winter's ravages and were able to survive outside all winter with no ill effects, even though I didn't take the time to move them to a safer location for protection, I won't have to do as much shopping next summer.

But please, make it just cold enough to kill all those creepy, annoying bugs, okay? Thanks.

And finally, on the subject of tweaks, could I ask you to employ just a few itty-bitty ones to some of the most loveable but troublesome plants in my garden? Could you please make it so ornamental grasses don't re-seed all over the dang place? And would you mind terribly making it so my lawn would stay green all summer without me having to painstakingly water it every single week, driving up the water bill to heights even the Rockefellers would complain about? And could you stunt the neighbor's invasive ivy vines so they would stop growing at around six inches instead of sixty feet? Oh, I'm so grateful.

And one last thing before I sign off. Pretty, pretty please make it so slugs hate the taste of Hosta leaves and aphids detest the juices of rose buds?

Okay that's all for now, Santa. I'll be sure to clean the chimney and leave you your favorite milk and cookies.

Sincerely,

Grace

Chapter Sixteen ~ My Advice for the Newbie

I think one of the things new gardeners might not understand is how much dedication it takes to become an expert at gardening. Like any endeavor, to become a garden authority and have the garden of your dreams requires extreme devotion. One must decide, at least for a time, to be completely enraptured by all things gardening, to eat, drink, and sleep gardening.

If you are fortunate enough to receive the bite of the gardening bug, it won't be painful as long as you hand over your wallet to your un-afflicted partner. It might itch at times, especially when it hasn't been exposed to sunlight for awhile, but at the onset, it will inject an elixir of sheer delight mixed with a crazed enthusiasm that has the potential to cause temporary blindness to all other endeavors.

It's the initial enjoyment that fuels the dedication. And then gives way to addiction. There are no twelve step meetings for gardeners. Why? Because there's not one garden addict that wants to give up the addiction. Not a one. Not when the fruit of the addiction is a prettier Earth.

There are a few guidelines that will make the intoxication all that much sweeter.

To become proficient requires a working knowledge of plants. This certainly doesn't happen instantly. Information, both print and picture to capture the eye, is easy to come by with the Internet at the ready. Further inquiry to local Horticultural Extension Services will reveal whether the plant is suitable to the local climate. I prefer to check with the Extension Service rather than local nurseries because, well, nurseries have a vested interest in selling plants. The Extension Service, on the other hand, is a science-based extension of the agricultural state university of the area. They have no bias and don't receive a commission. They will simply provide facts.

Studying various plant genera is nothing like being in school where studying was pure drudgery—at least, it was for me. Now, as an adult, studying is a self-imposed pleasure and a delightful way to interact with gardening peers, because eventually, we enjoy learning about the plants so much that we're emailing photos to our gardening buddies and figuring out ways we can both get our hands on the coveted specimen.

Eventually, I'm afraid, our beloved pursuit borders on obsession. In fact, for a lot of us, it skips right over the border while we are perusing the aisles of our twentieth plant sale of the season.

Plant sale. Those are two of my favorite words in the dictionary. And when they're lined up to form a phrase, they spike my adrenaline.

There is a thrill that comes with the discovery of a new plant. And that thrill is highly addictive. I'm no scientist but I'm pretty sure that scoring a yearned-after plant that perhaps has been scribbled on my wish list for the past few years releases a chemical in the brain. One that makes me dance happily, even in public places.

Mentors are helpful. One of the things a mentor does, besides providing priceless information and sharing their own plant treasures, is provide alerts to the choicest plant sales of the season. It is at those sales that great plants can be had at the best prices. Sometimes the specimens may not look as neat and tidy as the ones at the nursery, but as long as the roots are moist and get proper care, they'll do well.

It is not uncommon at the plant sales to observe people who appear to be wandering around in a daze. This is probably because they're tentative about purchasing a plant if it is very expensive, or not reliably winter-hardy, or, most critical, both of those things apply.

We'll read the tag several times while our mind bounces back and forth from images of our dwindling bank account balance—and how many days we'll be eating microwave popcorn before payday rolls around again—to the garden and how perfectly this particular plant would look there. If someone else shows an interest in this plant, we'll engage in friendly conversation but make it unequivocally clear that the plant is ours—at least until and if we make up our mind against purchasing it.

Having tuned out the murmur of a thousand other Die Hard gardeners at the plant sale, we continue to think and ponder and waffle. Just as we've almost made up our mind, another image whizzes into our consciousness.

It's dark, there's a strong East Wind. Sleet bites at our face. We're barefooted, or wearing our nearly worn-out flip flops, straining our back muscles in an effort to get that heavy pot indoors because Old Reliable, the weather guy, just mentioned the words "dropping below freezing tonight" on his evening forecast.

And then for just a split second we'll remember the horrific pain we felt last year when that freak cold front killed all of our supposedly winter-hardy New Zealand Flax.

We'll contemplate as to whether we want to make *even more* work for ourselves by growing another cold-sensitive plant. We've been thinking lately that we need to scale back and simplify. Maybe it would be better to play altruistic and leave this plant for some other sucker—I mean gardener. After all, it is the last one at this vendor's site and maybe that other gardener owns a heated greenhouse.

Okay, forget it, we think, suddenly needing coffee. As we back away, an image of *someone else* buying the plant pops into our head. Gardeners are very giving people, but only to a point.

Stepping in closer once again, we reach out and touch our beloved's incredible foliage, check the price once again and ... figure out how we're going to free our arms from the half dozen or so plants we're already carrying so we can retrieve our wallet and pay for the plant that has just, without uttering a word, talked us in to buying it.

While waiting for the cashier to give us our change, we're thinking about how delicious canned soup and popcorn taste.

This is how we deal with—I mean *enjoy*—the plant sale.

Once we've loaded the car with our plant purchases, we head for home with our fellow Die Hards who decided to honor our code of mutual enabling. By the time our partners in crime and their booty are all safely delivered to their respective homes, we have our plan of action pretty well figured out. We pull into the driveway and squint to see into the house to determine whether or not Life Partner is visible or not. Of course, we're hoping for the latter so we can, as stealthily as possible, haul our purchases out to the backyard before Life Partner sees us and we have to make up something quick like, "Oh, that? It's been here since April. You just now noticed it?"

Once everything is safely tucked into our secret holding area in the backyard and there is no sign that Life Partner is on the phone with the divorce lawyer, we tiptoe inside to pee and wash up, then to the kitchen to get something savory going for dinner because food does cover a multitude of sins and we're well aware that we're skating on thin ice right now.

The next day, after sufficiently placating our Life Partner in a multitude of ... um ... creative ways, our guilt hovers around a three on a one to ten scale. We've already promised ourselves that we will just *be happy* with what we have and not let ourselves be tempted to go to more plant sales or any of the nurseries that keep emailing us or posting alluring photos on Facebook. We've got chores to keep us busy in the garden and doing chores doesn't cost any money.

There ends the first principle of what newbie gardeners need to know to be successful.

Once you've got a good idea of what plants are all about, there is that nagging question of how to situate them in the garden. In other words, design. Gardeners must have a boatload of design prowess. It's *this* skill that allows us to do something remarkable with those irresistible plants we've brought home.

In layman's terms, we have to figure out where to put those beauties we couldn't resist at yesterday's sale. A keen eye for proper placement really helps. Knowing the needs of the plant—sun or shade, moist or dry soil—will also play a critical role in the decision-making process. However, only rarely do we discover the right spot on the first go around. We have to fiddle and experiment, then wait and see if the plant is happy in that spot. And there's not just one plant to find a spot for but, if we're lucky, a half dozen or so.

Sometimes, the plant we've just purchased—call it The Star—would look best in Spot A, but there's just one little problem: Plant A is already growing in Spot A. This means we have to play Musical Plants, and, since the neighbors seem hell-bent on blasting their music to the entire neighborhood, the challenge seems fitting.

The next step is deciding if Plant A is worthy of planting elsewhere or would be better off in the compost heap. There are several criteria that determine if a plant is worth keeping or not, the paramount one being *Do I like it?*

Say we do indeed like Plant A and decide to keep it. We dig it out of Spot A to make room for The Star. We get it planted, then while stepping back to observe it in its new home, trip and almost fall over the pot it came in, which we inadvertently tossed right in the pathway where we usually walk. Undeterred, we decide it looks great.

With that done, we begin the hunt for a new spot for Plant A, which, at present, is just a sad looking lumpy thing sitting in the wheelbarrow. We're pretty sure it wouldn't lean so much if it were given more sunlight so we decide on Spot B. But first we have to dig up and relocate Plant B from Spot B to make room for Plant A.

Sometimes we can play Musical Plants all day and into the evening, long after the neighbors have shut off their music and given the airwaves back to birdsong.

To the non-gardener, all of this may seem preposterous. They will believe that those of us who so bravely toil the soil are either slightly off kilter or brainwashed by some arcane retail marketing scheme. You have to walk a mile in a gardener's shoes before you can possibly understand the allure.

It's like this with any endeavor, especially creative ones that require a healthy amount of obsession and eccentricity to undertake. For the onlooker, it might be all too easy to judge the creator based on what we see as foolishness or craziness. But because we're observing from the outside, we can't possibly know the mind of the person and what drives them to do what they do.

I'm reminded of Mount Rushmore. I'm sure there were a hefty bunch of hecklers spouting off, naysayers, hypercritical spectators watching father and son Borglum hang by what must have looked like gossamer threads while engaged in the gargantuan task of manipulating solid granite into smooth presidential likenesses.

I would venture to guess that most, if not all, of the beautiful creations of man were conceived and carried out by slightly askew people, folks who were able to count the cost and were well aware of the risks and man hours involved. And who, driven by passion, ultimately determined that their project must be embarked upon.

I think we should applaud the eccentric and let them do their thing and see what kind of beauty will come of it.

Talent hits a target no one else can hit. Genius hits a target no one else can see.
~Arthur Schopenhauer

Chapter Seventeen ~ Life is Like a Lottery Ball

As a writer, I always take special notice when I encounter the talented and creative writing of my contemporaries. I love it—and get slightly jealous—when I read an especially entertaining combination of words. Yes, I'm a word nerd. I still have a lot to learn but I'm enjoying the process.

Recently I saw a cleverly executed simile. It went something like "another scenario will pop up like a lottery ball." The bouncing lottery ball, enmeshed in chaotic swirling with its rivals until randomly caught in some kind of snare and brought to the forefront for keen observation. I love it.

Life's many concerns can be likened to the fate of lottery balls. Our comings and goings are tossed around by a demanding calendar full of imperatives. We try to forge some kind of schedule to keep control and familiarity, rising at the same hour every morning, bouncing through our routine until the clock reminds us that we'd better hit the hay because tomorrow will demand a similar performance.

Like those chaotic balls that seem to be tamable only one at a time, if we're paying attention, we can grab hold of one aspect of our life and examine it closely. However, we should never delude ourselves into thinking we can have everything under control or all figured out. We can't. We have to live with a certain level of unknowing. We either have to ignore those things we have no control over or, better yet, conjure up a measure of faith that things are moving in the right direction, and, if our motivations are on the up and up, that the outcomes will ultimately be for the positive.

The older I get, the more I realize how much I *don't* know about things. However, the more I learn and the longer I'm alive, the more at peace I feel with *not* having all the answers.

People afflicted with anxiety like to control things. They believe they can ease their anxiety by being completely aware of every situation and the ramifications of each. They attempt to manipulate the outcome in their favor. They need to have their fingers in many pots and are adept at wearing many hats because no one can do the job better than they can. Onlookers often label them *control freaks*.

When I was younger, I was a control freak par excellence due to my anxiety issues. As much as I hate to admit it now, I really thought I could control, among other things, my garden. I thought that if I just made sure all the weeds were pulled and all the top-heavy plants were sufficiently tied, my world would be perfect.

I wonder why we human beings feel the need to appear perfect for the world. Is it a sign of weakness to admit our imperfections? I don't think so. In fact, I'm much more comfortable being in the presence of people who can readily admit their shortcomings and, better yet, laugh about them.

My garden is shamefully full of imperfections and I've yet to visit a garden that's perfect, although I've been to several that are damn close. Gardens by their very nature can't be perfect because they're always in flux as plants ebb and flow. Granted, there is a moment of perfection for each plant but rarely do those occur simultaneously.

How lovely my climbing Cecile Brunner rose was one year. A French rose of the *Polyantha* class, it was introduced into commerce in 1881; I loved the idea of growing a plant with such a prodigious history. It scrambled up and wove its way in and out of the rustic log arbor my son had built for me. Bearing hundreds of miniature, spicy-scented pink roses, it was the picture of loveliness. Perfection. I basked in its charm and took lots of photos and thought of myself as a gardener extraordinaire. I even started talking in a fake British accent. French was too difficult.

It all looked so elegant and grand, but only for about a week. Then came the petal-fall period. Although pink buds continued to unfold into pretty blossoms, the aging flowers were wilting and forlorn and ruining the vignette. What was worse, the entire area was carpeted in dull pink and browning petals that reminded me of wet confetti. My need for perfection was causing me extreme distress.

I think it was then that I finally conceded to the fact that my garden would never become the ideal I witnessed in those glossy photographs in the books and magazines that filled my shelves. The concept was a misnomer, a myth, propagated by stellar and timely photographers and skilled publishers. It was a cruel conspiracy aimed at the vulnerable, control freak gardeners of the world—people like me.

No garden books or magazines publish photos of the garden at its worst. You never see photos of the muddy patio or the broken birdhouse. The photographer is nowhere to be found when weeds invade the lawn and slugs eat the dephiniums.

Nature plays a huge part in correcting our delusions of perfection and control. Petals must fall. Weeds must grow. Wind must swirl around and knock branches loose.

Working *with* nature rather than trying to manipulate it into something we see in those magazines might actually work for a while. But it won't last.

Both gardening and life will drive us crazy if we're constantly endeavoring to control all the lottery balls. Instead, if we have fun and enjoy those fleeting perfect instants, if we remember they're momentary—and take lots of photos—we won't be so depressed when the whole place looks a mess.

Chapter Eighteen ~ Aster Anarchy and Bachelor Button Bedlam

I've got lots of familiar garden inhabitants. Most of them are dear friends. I talk to them when they awaken in the spring. I smile when they start blooming. I grab my camera and take too many photos. My plants are like family to me. I appreciate their familiarity and continuity and their persistence and staying power.

It would break my heart if certain plants were to relocate to that great compost heap in the sky. My Indigo Bush shrub is one. It's not just the adorable lavender pea-like flowers, but the soft pinnate foliage that accompanies them. And catching a whiff of honeysuckle or plucking a raspberry is pure bliss. I love all my Clematis vines. I couldn't begin to think what my garden would be like without Garden Phlox blooming in late July and perfuming my bedside. Or my Daphne blooming in February. Or my roses blooming sporadically all season long.

Sometimes familiar plants get the short end of the stick. Weeds are a no-brainer, of course. I will always have a bias against the dandelion, unless it somehow magically starts bearing pink flowers. Until then, I will continue to give it the heave-ho.

The familiar garden plants, on the other hand, require a bit more contemplation. They're a lot like that trendy outfit I bought just because it was trendy, wore a few times, then relegated to the back of the closet while mumbling something like, "What was I thinking?"

I often wandered through my garden muttering that very same question. But recently I've decided to rethink my attitude towards the familiar plants growing in my borders. The perennial aster, a purple daisy-like wildflower in many parts of the United States, can surely be classified as common, familiar. But it has its merits: *It grows and it blooms.*

Years ago, I received a sizeable clump of purple asters from a gardening friend. Immensely grateful for her generosity, I brought it home and quickly and lovingly planted it. Not only did that clump grow, it grew expeditiously. The plant should have come with a warning label that read: My goal is to take over the world.

Because it did so well, I figured, "Heck, why not divide it several times and plant it all over the entire garden?"

A few years later, there were close to thirty clumps of asters in various places in my garden, as I continued to dig, divide, and increase my supply. I really wasn't thinking about the fact that I was encouraging a monster.

It wasn't much later that familiarity set in and I grew bored and contemptuous. I wanted a new outfit.

With precious little garden space and a longing for something new and exciting and *pink*, the asters were dug and given to unsuspecting garden friends. Despite my efforts, I can never dig out the entire clump and always, without fail, a few roots remain and, by the following year, morph into yet another good-sized clump.

The common aster continued to co-exist with the more exotic this or that—not a bad combination most of the time since asters really are good mixers. But a persistent fear nagged me. Would the Underground Aster Operation succeed in an all-out occupation of my garden? I kept pulling the telltale purple stems as I saw them; maybe I was actually making a difference.

Once, while holding a freshly dug aster clump destined for the yard debris can, a clever idea popped into my head. Since asters seem to be oblivious to the extremes, doing well in both shade and wet soil or full sun and dry soil and everything in between, why not plant my cast-off clumps in a particularly difficult area of the garden, one of those spots where nothing grows?

I did just that ... and they grew. So now I'm letting asters have their way in those places while I continue to dig them out of the garden proper. I'm feeling rather smug about my problem-solving prowess.

The aster invasion forestalled, I turned my attention to another all too familiar problem plant, the perennial Bachelor Button. Smart gardeners will eradicate this plant from their borders in a hurry once they observe its cunning nature, as it goes about its insurrection by seeding everywhere.

I couldn't seem to act like a smart gardener. I was smitten with those unique spidery pinwheel petals of purest indigo spiraling into a puffy purple center. And when I put my nose close to it, a sweet, subtle fragrance sealed the deal. True blue flowers are uncommon; these would start blooming in late February in my garden.

My original idea was to mimic my garden blogger buddy Barry Vanderveer and his love of blue flowers by sectioning off a spot for an all-blue-flowered border. I had high hopes. It would boast a succession of azure blooms from late winter with the aforementioned perennial bachelor buttons and finish it off in mid fall with hardy plumbago. It would be a challenging task, given the rarity of the true blue bloomers I had to work with, but, in my ignorance, I thought I could get it to happen. Besides, I knew Barry was just an email away.

It didn't work. My blue border was a bust. For one thing, Barry's blue flowers were being lovingly tended in shade and moist soil, while mine were being tortured in heavy clay and six hours of scorching sun.

Everything except the bachelor button died during the first year, probably torturous deaths, as well, given that I had unwittingly asked them to duke it out with a very tyrannical bachelor button genus that clearly was not a good neighbor. That could explain why it's still a bachelor.

My next brilliant idea was to give the bachelor buttons the entire border, if they promised to behave themselves and stay within their allotted space. But, of course, they weren't too keen on this arrangement. They're bachelors, after all. Without any neighbors to elbow up to, they were kind of lonely and miserable. Finally, because I had a mini-nursery of plants waiting for a chance to dazzle me, I yanked out the bachelor buttons, thus ending the all-blue phase of my gardening career.

I've concluded that some plants have a mind of their own and like, a temperamental toddler, are determined to do it their way, often to their own demise.

There have been times when I've felt a combination of annoyance and humiliation at the way some of my proposed plans have played out. But I've moved beyond all of that, and it seems small in retrospect.

I guess when we're younger, every quandary seems immense and insurmountable. At times, we can see no way at all out of our troubles but somehow we muddle through and move on. Then when we're down the road a ways and have a little more perspective, we look back and realize that what we thought was so gargantuan was really not all that big of a deal.

This doesn't mean that every conflict is no big deal or that we're overreacting by believing it's insurmountable. Some events are nothing short of catastrophic. But even those challenges are often temporary. We move through them and beyond, continuing down the road a little wiser and, hopefully, a little gentler on ourselves and those around us.

Chapter Nineteen ~ On Fitting a Square Peg into a Round Hole

Basic gardening is about combining two major skills: understanding and catering to each individual plant's specific needs and creating an environment within which they can all live in harmony.

Gardening is a lot like jewelry making. My oldest daughter is incredibly skilled at creating necklaces, bracelets, and earrings using beads. When embarking on a new project, the first thing she'll do is decide what individual beads she'd like to use. She'll choose them by color and size and consider how they'll fit to create a harmonious piece. Then she'll choose a type of wire to string them on to. When she shows me her finished project, it always makes me gasp in amazement—dozens of little elements, conjoined to create one masterpiece.

This is how gardening works, too. Lots of plants, each with its own role to play, make up one masterpiece: the garden.

During garden touring season, you'll instinctively know when you've stepped foot in a garden that is missing one of the two skills. You'll either be enveloped in a jungle of amazing plants with no form or definition guiding you, or you'll be in awe of brilliant hardscape with nary a plant to be seen. In both cases, you'll be dissatisfied with the experience.

I believe I possess a moderate proficiency in both skills. I am a decent plant-chooser and a decent plant-placer.

However, let me be clear. I am *not* stellar at either skill, evidenced by the fact that I'm constantly playing Musical Plants, that desperate game where Plant A is dug up from Spot A to make room for the freshly purchased Star which leaves displaced Plant A to be attended to, resulting in the search for Spot B, which frequently means displacing Plant B … that's me, the queen of plant-moving.

One remedy to Musical Plants is purchasing hefty pots and Costco-sized bags of potting soil. Some might call this cheating but desperate measures call for ingenuity. I have a lot of plants in hefty containers. In a lot of ways they're easier to care for than plants in the garden proper. For one thing, they're closer to the water faucet.

My garden proper is very tricky. It's got to do with the climate. Never mind that I've lived in western Oregon for the better part of five decades, I'm still unpleasantly surprised when the middle of August roles around and the ground, waterlogged for nine months, has mysteriously morphed into Pueblo clay. The plants along the east-facing fence, farthest from the hose of course, suffer greatly.

One of the reasons this problem exists is because I'm doing what I'm supposed to do and planting in the month of May which, if you know western Oregon, is still the rainy season. Everything is possible in May, especially when you've got a faulty memory and a healthy load of denial. In May the gardener doesn't remember what the garden was like during last August's rivalry with New Mexico. It's May, so I situate that thirsty plant out yonder in thick, heavy, waterlogged soil, mix in a little compost thinking it will actually help, and leave the poor thing to fend for itself. But that's because I'm not thinking about both principles. I'm thinking about the *design* but not about the needs of the plant.

I've spent many, many Mays not thinking like both a plant-chooser and a plant-placer, neurotically forcing that square peg into a round hole. It makes more work for me in the long run as, come August, I'm discouraged and annoyed with hauling around an overly kinky hose with a leaky nozzle, getting soaked in a futile effort to prolong May and "water until well-established."

Following directions is always much easier on paper where everything is fairly straightforward and cut and dried, where the multitude of variables are blatantly missing from the equation. Easy. Fit this peg in this hole. Water, step back, and enjoy.

Life, on the other hand, isn't that simple. I'm convinced that the Creator of the universe uses life's various mysteries to confound us, to remind us that we don't know squat about anything, to show us that it takes more than pat answers to figure out a quandary. It takes a multitude of skills, like teamwork and cooperation and patience to put into place that beloved ideal and then nurture it to fulfillment and beyond.

I suppose if everything went smoothly all the time, we'd get bored and cocky. Perhaps the challenges do more than sharpen our skills. They keep us humble.

Chapter Twenty ~ When Rhyme and Reason Elude Us

Anyone who's been gardening for any length of time or watches the evening news on occasion is aware of the ongoing issues concerning invasive species. The environmental impact of an out-of-control invader could be devastating to various ecosystems. I'm very grateful that we have diligent watchdog groups on the prowl, making sure nothing slips by them, barking when they spot a stranger.

As serious as the global impact of invasives could become, when the subject is funneled and squeezed and parsed down to the level of *my* garden and what impact *my* actions have on the environment, I have to laugh. It's not that I'm impervious to responsible gardening, it's just that, well, my garden isn't exactly the type that supports invasive anything. Just the opposite. It's keeping things *alive* that's the real challenge for me.

Take mint, for instance. When we moved here in 1997, one of the first plants I got in the ground was my pot of Orange Mint. It has a heavenly fragrance and I admit to having more than a slight obsession with fragrant plants. I stood back and watched. It thrived and spread and just about the time I uttered an unholy, "Holy Shit, what have I done?" the entire swath died for lack of summer water.

And take the devilish Purple Loosestrife. In other locales it is loathed and despised and vilified for choking waterways and displacing indigenous plants. Me, well, I've got two clumps of it growing in my garden. Never has it spread. Never has it seeded. My soil is too dry for root-spread and deadheading is an easy rite of summer. I wish my Loosestrife *would* spread, just a little.

In some parts of the country Heavenly Bamboo is invasive, thanks to birds who eat the berries then deposit them on fertile soil. Not in my garden. The birds around here turn up their noses at the berries on my plants, so it grows as slow as slow, which suits me just fine.

Even the universally scorned variegated Bishop's Weed is fairly well-behaved in my garden. And Bugle Weed, which seems to be a prolific spreader in other gardens, I call *Bungle* Weed because it has sufficiently botched its reputation in mine.

Creeping Jenny has earned the pejorative, *Creepy* Jenny because of her wayward tendencies. She enjoys my ponds, but other than that she has not been terribly willful in my garden.

Conversely, Blue Star Creeper, which is not on any governmental watchdog invasive list as far as I know, seems to *really* favor my garden. I brought my first pot home about ten years ago. It spread, and at its current stage, has migrated cunningly to the perennial beds, refusing to grow where I planted it but thriving everywhere it shouldn't.

Cypress Spurge also grows all over my garden. I love its soft little stems that remind me of miniature pine trees. If it weren't so cute, I'd dig it out. In spring when it blooms it smells nice, and I'm a sucker for fragrance.

The home gardener is fairly limited in how they can impact the global environment, especially where invasive plants are concerned. But staying diligent to our little slice of earth can certainly keep it from being overrun with bully plants. In fact, I believe it's imperative. For example, I grow Bronze Fennel because I love the wispy, puce-colored foliage and how the bees flock to the flowers. It feels very gratifying to contribute to the health and vigor of our resident pollinator population. However, I've learned through a series of hard knocks that I cannot allow its flowers to go to seed. If I do, I'll have five million baby plants the following year. Ditto for chives.

And don't allow any of the pretty Ornamental Oreganos to go to seed, either, unless you're planning on digging up several hundred progeny for all your gardening friends and all your friends' friends and all of their friends. You'll run out of friends long before you run out of plants. You might lose a few, too.

A quick Internet search will provide a vast amount of up-to-the-minute information on invasive plants and animals for specific regions. It will also explain why certain species are on that list to begin with and what kind of threat they pose. While our backyard gardens may not be contributing to the problem, it's a good idea to be aware and do what we can to minimize any impact.

Mostly, the interlopers in my garden are the typical weeds of western Oregon: bitter cress, dandelion and that tenacious, yet pretty bronze-leaved, yellow-flowered oxalis.

As much as I despise the little buggers, I'll take them over scary things, like Alligator Weed and Skunk Vine that are on the loose in Florida. Or Swallow Warts growing wild in California, or Mile-a-Minute Weed, an escapee chewing up West Virginia.

***

I'm aware of that old "the grass is greener" lie. I'm pretty sure the grass isn't greener on the other side of anywhere. It's the same grass. You won't hear me complain about the idiosyncrasies of western Oregon, wishing I could uproot and transplant to another, more hospitable locale. I recognize how good I've got it despite my plethora of failures and the seemingly never-ending dry season.

Speaking of failures, recently I looked over the plant list I keep on my computer for quick reference. Scrolling through, I realized that, over the years, I've killed a heck of a lot of plants. My notes say things like: "housed in a container, a freak cold snap was its undoing, and "housed under the patio roof for protection, I neglected to water it." There are a sprinkling of "who knows?" And one "I don't remember ever growing this." There are other notes, as well, since this is a sixteen-page, size ten font, single spaced list. Some of the notes aren't very complimentary about my skills and/or intelligence. But losing a plant happens to the best of us.

Plants have a mind of their own. This is what I say when plants don't perform like they're supposed to. They either grow too big or they completely die without explanation. Or they're alive all right, but their once-variegated leaves have, overnight, completely reverted to solid green. Or they bloom in a completely different color than the tag and the cute nursery guy described. Or they are purported to be drought tolerant but get pissed off, curl up, and croak on the first dry day of the season.

But all of these are the exception. Most plants will perform wonderfully for us. Plants aim to please and have no ax to grind. I believe plants *want* to grow. They're wired to thrive and, given the right conditions, they do. Most of my plants have never even considered breaking my heart. They're much too devoted to me to do such a horrid thing. They love me and I love them. I take care of them and they thank me by wowing me with their foliage and flowers.

If I notice a plant performing poorly, and if it's not too big, I might dig it up and put it in a pot for a while or move it to a more suitable location. Trial and error. Sometimes the diagnosis will be simple, other times, not so much.

Despite how challenging it can be, it's still *much* easier to diagnose a plant's conundrums than a person's emotional conundrums.

A plant will frequently be cooperative enough to show us what it needs. Wilting foliage, for instance will often reveal a need for water. A plant leaning towards sunlight is saying that it needs more sunshine.

Diagnosing people, as smart as we'd like to think we are, makes plant-diagnosing seem like a cakewalk. We're a complicated species, and often clueless about how to correctly diagnose and treat the human behavior we're confronted with. We want to be careful not to pigeonhole, but we're often unable to resist that nagging temptation to jump right in and offer advice that maybe isn't warranted. Usually our motivation is to help—but sometimes it's to get them to shut up and go away.

I confess that I tended toward this with my teenage daughters who, unlike my son, had more than their share of histrionic moments. My recipe was to dish out my advice in copious quantities. Of course, they didn't always digest it too well and generally threw it up in my face. Eventually I learned that what they wanted from me was a listening, compassionate ear, not a plateful of platitudes.

Chapter Twenty-One ~
The Human Club

Like many people, the bulk of my gardening time is spent in solitude. I prefer it that way. Being by myself sparks my creative juices and allows them to flow uninhibited, bouncing from this idea to that next job, back and forth. Being disconnected from humanity provides a very special link to my creative side, even if it's for just a few minutes. It's all very therapeutic and fun.

I like to imagine my kids will someday have gardens of their own. Two of my young adult offspring will sometimes visit me while I'm deadheading roses or loading the wheelbarrow or picking raspberries. They aren't interested in helping me, because to them it's still *work*, but I know eventually, when they have their own garden, they will see that, although it is indeed work, it's creative work.

***

When my youngest daughter entered middle school, I decided I wanted to become official. I wanted my bio to say a little more than simply the derogatory Lifetime Student at the School of Hard Knocks. Although I still relished my alone time in the garden, I was ready to be affiliated with something garden-related. I pondered going back to school to earn a horticulture degree but that seemed like a bigger step than I was ready to take. Fortunately, there was another option. I enrolled in the Master Gardener Program through the Oregon State University Extension Service.

The Master Gardener classes took place in winter, during the non-gardening months, which was perfect. It would have seemed silly to be *indoors* learning about gardening during any other time of the year.

As a visual, hands-on, learn-by-doing sort of gal, I wondered how I would fare in such an academic environment. Images of my traumatic teenage years flashed through my mind and attempted to dissuade me from returning to a venue in which I failed so miserably decades before.

But I needn't have worried. The classroom was full of people just like me: plant people, eager to learn the principles of smart gardening and the reasons why certain garden practices were beneficial and others were proven obsolete with the latest research.

I felt right at home and quickly made friends as we listened to lectures on raised beds and soils and critters and the seemingly countless ways our poor plants were vulnerable to imminent death and destruction.

To be honest, being immersed in horticultural horrors for six-hours a day for ten weeks was daunting, but fascinating. When we consider the multitude of unique processes that must align perfectly to make a healthy plant and a robust ecosystem, it's pretty miraculous. And if mishaps occur, which they do, the Master Gardener course taught the best ways to deal with them.

After graduating we were expected to work the call-in desk, answering whatever horticultural question a caller might have. I did most of my volunteering during the month of May when the questions about growing tomato plants were at their pinnacle. I'd relay what I was taught and hope that my nervous fumbling of words didn't cause too much confusion.

It wasn't long after graduating with my Master Gardener certificate that Barb Fick, OSU's horticulturist and all around delightful person, introduced me to Gloria Clark, another delightful person who was, and still is, the head reporter for *Northwest Boomer & Senior News*. She interviewed me for a series of articles she was writing on gardeners in the area. It wasn't much longer until Gloria introduced me to her editor-in-chief, Trude Crow, who offered me the garden columnist writing gig for *NW Boomer & Senior News*. I'll take it!

***

A few years later, I became better acquainted with Carol, a neighbor who takes gardening to a higher level than I do. Viewing her extraordinary, well kept, neat-as-a-pin garden is incredibly inspiring. I usually get really sleepy when I visit because her garden is so relaxing.

Carol has a penchant for plant placement, and, with almost an acre to garden, her plants have plenty of room to reach their potential, uninhibited by pushy neighboring plants.

For the past several years, Carol and I have visited nurseries and allowed ourselves to get caught up in the thrill of the hunt. We always leave with something new and exciting to add to our already bustling gardens. Having a likeminded gardener-friend like Carol in my life is a treasured gift.

I met Lynda through Carol. Lynda is another plant-savvy pal. She gardens on a slope with an incredible view of the Willamette Valley, which stretches for miles to the east. She loves to grow new plants from seed so I always try to save a few to pass along.

About the time I became acquainted with Lynda, I launched my garden blog. It was slow going at first because I wasn't acquainted with any garden bloggers and no one knew my blog was out there on the Internet.

After a few months with no success, it occurred to me to Google Garden Blog Directories. I realized right off that belonging to a directory was the way to get noticed and meet fellow garden bloggers. I applied for membership to several. *Blotanical* was and remains one of the most active, and through my membership I've met a great number of really wonderful gardeners from around the globe, people with not just amazing garden talents but excellent photography and writing skills, as well.

One of the friends I made through mutual blogging is Annie. When I saw the photos of her amazing gardens, I was hooked. It was a wonderful surprise to discover that Annie and I lived in the same town and that she is also a Master Gardener. We've been friends ever since.

Last year Annie, Carol, Lynda, and several other phenomenal gardeners in the area launched a garden group that I'm privileged to be a part of. We meet once a month to share our mutual gardening victories and woes.

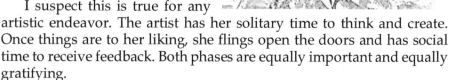

Humans are social creatures. Woven within our DNA is this mysterious need for camaraderie and connection. We fancy others observing our creations and appreciating our efforts. We like to discourse on the hows and whys of what we do. We like to learn and we like it when other people learn from us.

I suspect this is true for any artistic endeavor. The artist has her solitary time to think and create. Once things are to her liking, she flings open the doors and has social time to receive feedback. Both phases are equally important and equally gratifying.

Gardening is one of the creative ways to find balance in life. I think it gets easier with experience, age, and understanding and accepting our own unique proclivities. And the more time we spend sharing those proclivities with others, the more we find how much alike we are in this club called being human.

Chapter Twenty-Two ~
Garden Consulting

Soon after I finished the OSU Master Gardener course in 2002, I began working at a small start-up nursery. I was acquainted with the owners through my daughters' school. Nice people, but not very plant savvy.

Getting the nursery job was on the heels of my admittedly half-hearted attempt to get my daughters' school principal to hire me. I had a vision for restoring the school's weed-infested courtyard gardens into something that the children could enjoy. But the principal was reticent to communicate with me. Maybe it was my desire for financial compensation. Maybe I annoyed him. Maybe he just didn't like gardens. I'll never know.

Fortunately, I impressed the nursery owners and they seemed pleased to bring me on board. I remember the first day, seeing the heaping mess on what I assumed was intended to be a checkout counter. Upturned, half-dead plants were sharing space with opened, soil-stained reference books and seed catalogs. Stacks of nursery pots rested horizontally with bits of potting soil decorating everything like sprinkles on a cupcake. My first order of business, I decided, would be to clear off this work space, thinking that the owners—and customers—would be pleased to have a central, unencumbered checkout location.

Other than the piercing pain of a sliver inside my fingernail, I managed to complete the task without any mishaps. A smug sense of satisfaction followed. But the mess reappeared after I took a day off. I think that should have been my first clue.

It was June when I started working at the nursery. July ushered in the dry season, which meant keeping the plants watered was my paramount task. Hauling a heavy, leaky hose between endless, crooked rows of black nursery pots in ninety degree weather proved to be less than a delightful experience. Day in and day out, the bottom half of my jeans would become heavily water-soaked. My tennis shoes were a wet magnet for you name it. My spirits were as dampened as the top layer of soil on the plants I tried, in many cases, fruitlessly to keep alive. But I kept at it because the owners felt confident about leaving me in charge. Not only did it feel good to have them trust me, I liked the independence.

My biggest anxiety came from my brain's insistent rendering of a fatal crash on Highway 20 just a few steps from the nursery's entrance. This stretch of highway, which connected the two largest towns of the area, was notorious for accidents. It was a narrow strip and on the opposite side was a steep drop off to the river below. Although it was posted at forty-five miles an hour, people routinely ignored such trivialities and would also neglect to heed the brake lights ahead of them until it was too late. While engaged in nursery tasks, I kept an unhealthy watch on the motorized comings and goings, praying that the worst wouldn't happen. I get queasy at the sight of blood.

The owners were good people but, as I said, not very plant savvy. They appreciated my knowledge with constant queries that I was happy to answer. Customers were far and few between; I had my theories as to why we failed to attract the masses. I believed it was due in part to the newness of the nursery and because about four miles due west stood one of the most impressive plant nurseries in the entire valley. Our prices were more wallet-friendly, comparatively speaking, but the nursery down the way was an impressive mega-store. It's not easy to compete with that.

I thoroughly enjoyed visiting with the customers who braved their way along the highway-of-imagined-death and into the store. Plant people are a delightful bunch, although sometimes a bit cryptic with their demands.

"I need a plant," a nicely dressed middle-aged woman would declare after the mutual weather pleasantries were finalized.

"Well," I'd say, harboring a tiny bit of dread at what I knew was coming, "would you like some help or would you prefer to look around a while?"

"Well, I'm looking for a plant to go next to the garage," she'd say, wistfully scanning the area and lightly touching a nearby petunia blossom.

I'd wait to see if she was planning to elaborate or traipse off to look. Invariably, she would elaborate, but only slightly. "We had some work done and now the spot is bare."

The murky waters were slowly clearing, but still stubbornly muddy. She wanted my assistance but she couldn't communicate very well.

So began my litany of questions. "Well, what kind of sun exposure does this area get? Sun or shade? What is the soil like? Is it dry or wet? Do you have automatic sprinklers? And how wide and tall is the area?"

Once the location specifics were established, I would launch into the more subjective inquiries. "So what kind of plant are you looking for?"

"Well, something pretty," she'd say.

Disguising either my chuckle or my eyeball roll, depending on my mood, I go on. "Do you want a tree, a shrub, a groundcover? How tall do you want it to be? Do you want it to look good year round? Can it be deciduous or would you prefer an evergreen?"

"Oh, no. I don't want a Christmas tree," she'd say, causing me to regret using the word *evergreen* without the clarifying *broadleaf* preceding it. To most people, evergreen is synonymous with conifer.

"Um, well we have a few shrubs that keep their leaves all winter over here," I'd say, pointing to what vaguely represented an intended grouping of plants. I didn't want to tell her that the owner was not only a packrat but also possessed very mysterious organizational skills. I just let her assess the plants I pointed out while I stealthily looked around to see if I could locate the rest of the broadleaf evergreen shrubs.

"Oh, please watch your step over here," I'd tell her, mortified at the mess and smell the owner left while engaged in some puzzling task of apparently major significance the day prior.

The customers were always so nice about that kind of thing. If they were as mortified as I was, they kept it to themselves. However, when many of them would mistakenly assume I was the owner of the nursery, I was *extremely* quick to put that thought to rest. I didn't want anyone to think these were *my* messes.

Sometimes the browsing customer would find a plant that suited her and go ahead and make a purchase. But I wouldn't let it bother me if they didn't. Plant shopping is highly subjective and personal. It's a lot like buying underwear. People have their biases and preferences. I can respect that.

Still, it was a little daunting when every single plant I would suggest was met with a frown and two thumbs way down.

"How about a Crape Myrtle?" I'd say, lifting a pot containing the nicest looking specimen of the twenty or so we had in stock.

"Oh, no. I don't like that." She'd say without even knowing that it bloomed. "The leaves will blow inside the garage and make a mess."

Something told me this customer would be leaving without a plant and with two thumbs pointing to China.

Another challenge I often encountered was when the customer knew which plant he wanted but had no idea what it was.

"Hi. Can I help you?" I'd say cheerfully, wiping my grubby hands on a fresh paper towel from the roll I just found hiding behind the shelf, thankfully still wrapped in its packaging.

"Hi. Yes. I want one of those plants with the purple flowers," he'd say in all earnestness.

After the first few dozen times I was confronted with this, I had my inquest memorized. "Is it blooming right now?" I'd ask with a cheerful smile.

If he answered in the affirmative, it would narrow the options considerably. What I dreaded was when he'd answer with, "Um, no. It blooms in, let's see, August or June ... it was around Hal's birthday," he'd mumble, trying to think.

Now I could just suggest he grab his smart phone, Google purple-flowered plants that bloom in July, and come back with a name while I help this other customer who is about to trip over a bucket of peat moss. But back in the dark ages we had to do things the old fashioned way.

I'd grab the musty reference books, and, after brushing off as much soil and unidentifiable detritus as possible, I'd hand one to him and thumb through the other one, wracking my brain. I was as curious as he by then. Maybe a bit more annoyed, but still interested.

I have tremendous respect for the garden coaches or consultants of the world. It is not an easy job. Let me rephrase that. Aspects of the job are not easy. The plant part is a breeze compared to the human part.

Working at the nursery was not only mentally challenging at times but physically demanding all the time. With no place to sit except a comfy overturned five-gallon bucket, I was usually on my feet during the entire shift. And as the weather went from warm and wistful to wet and windy, I got used to being perpetually chilled. I also got used to seeing my breath when I spoke. I got used to listening to conservative talk shows on a crackly portable radio. I got used to water dripping right beside an electrical outlet. I got used to tripping over hoses. I got used to moldy plants and wind slapping against the roof of the greenhouse.

Sometimes we turn down a road and start driving without a clue as to where we'll end up. The view isn't too bad although questions like What am I doing this for? loom on the periphery. The questions don't really sync up with answers. We're just on the road and feel as though it's important to be there. That there is significance that will someday make itself known and all we can do is trust that. This is how I felt about my one-year stint at a plant nursery. I learned a lot while I traveled that road, but when I approached the fork, I knew it was time to veer left and let a new road take me somewhere else. I don't think the owners ever really understood my reasons for leaving. I'm not sure I do, either.

Chapter Twenty-Three ~ When Plants Are Like Children

Through the years, I've become more observant and less inclined to make hasty assumptions about things. When I do make an assumption, I'm quick to recognize it as such and not take it as an indisputable fact.

This principle is applicable when dealing people, especially children. Keen observation and careful interpretation are vital to healthy, harmonious relationships. I made that up but I believe it's true.

There are ways to interpret the moods of children. The poker hand of life is not all that difficult to read. A frown, a terse comment, arms folded across the chest, stomping off with a heavy sigh, these are just a few obvious tells. Most kids aren't very skilled at concealing their hand.

But sometimes children do things that seem peculiar, that make us scratch our head and wonder if we're raising a healthy kid or if we need to administer some tough love. We want to know what is normal. It can be heartbreaking when things don't make sense.

Plants have tells, too, all non-verbal, of course. When a plant is happy, it'll be obvious by its growth and vigor, its pretty flowers, and a scent as sweet as its disposition. And when that plant *isn't* happy, the signs of impending doom will also be obvious.

An obvious plant tell occurs when my Japanese Forest Grass gets thirsty. Like a three-year-old making excuses before bedtime, my plants make their water wishes known by curling their slender blades in on themselves until the whole clump looks like thin talons reaching for the water faucet. It's quite dramatic.

But, just like parenting, it can be tricky when plants do weird things and we don't know if the actions are standard behavior or not.

For instance, a plant that drops all its leaves during the growing season is usually a plant in peril, except that some leaf-drop is completely normal. I bought my lovely Arbutus years ago with the idea that a broadleaf evergreen shrub would look fabulous in one particular spot in my garden. What I didn't realize at the time was that although Arbie rightly kept the majority of his leaves during the winter months, he has the annoying habit of dropping his older leaves year round. *Year round!* Arbie is lush and green from the knees up. But look down at his feet and it's perpetual autumn.

Given two choices, I figured I could either tolerate Arbie's idiosyncracies, hoping he'd grow out of it, or I could give him up for adoption. The latter was out of the question. So, like any good mother— or gardener—I decided I'd adapt and do what I could to help him thrive.

After twelve years, I have to confess that my behavior modification sermons aren't having the slightest effect. The foliage still falls. I do, however, cut out all of the older bits, the equivalent of cleaning his room, in parenting terms.

As with children, there are degrees of plant peril. Some issues can be ignored, such as my pear tree's foliar mystery that I should remember from my Master Gardener training but don't. Since it doesn't seem to adversely affect the tree's ability to produce fruit, I just ignore it. I liken it to the horticultural equivalent to a bad case of acne—a bit unsightly, but not life-threatening.

Other times, the issue is something easily remedied. Like when I discover aphids on my plants, I shoot water at them. Aphids are soft-bodied bugs. I remember *that* from my Master Gardener training. I just shoot them with water or squish them with my fingers if I'm wearing gloves. They die without my having to administer any big guns in the form of poison.

Sometimes, especially during my early years, I was pretty adept at putting my needs before those of my plants. It wouldn't matter if the tag said to plant this baby in shade. I'd plant it where I thought it would look best.

This kind of thing can happen with kids, too. Sometimes, as their caretakers, we can wittingly or unwittingly manipulate them. Even though we think we know best, what we're doing is steering them towards *our* goals and losing sight of what their needs and wishes are. They might comply at first because they want to make us happy, but eventually their true colors will reveal themselves. They'll turn brown. They'll wilt and look very sad.

Being able to decipher a plant's issues requires skills right up there with the ones Kenny Rodgers sings about. We have to know when to hold and when to fold.

There are times when I need to walk away, such as when I realize that growing Scotch Moss between my pathway pavers just isn't going to happen. And when I delude myself into thinking I can successfully grow tropical plumeria flowers, I need to run.

Eventually our kids grow up and mature and grow roots. They produce oodles of shiny leaves and they blossom and make us proud. We feel relief that the plants we've labored over for years and years have settled in and are happy. And that's when we know we've been good people-gardeners.

Chapter Twenty-Four ~ You Don't Know Until You Try

Any gardener will tell you that gardening is, by and large, an exercise of trial and error—frequently a lot of error, at least in the beginning. Then, when we manage to get a few successes under our belts, we're inspired to go a little crazy and try new things and, before you know it, the entire backyard is transformed into a botanical oasis. That's exactly how it unfolded for me.

Success is a powerful motivator—and not just in the garden. If you cook a delicious meal, you feel motivated to buy that cookbook and expand your horizons. If you make friends with the gal in accounting, you feel inspired to be friendly with the receptionist. Success in whatever area we achieve it inspires us and builds our confidence.

Despite my often impetuous practices, I've had multiple successes in the garden. This is why it's jam-packed with plants. It's never been dubbed an oasis, but its close cousin, jungle, is about right.

In a way, I'm addicted to success and the feeling it gives me. When I witness my Cinco de Mayo rosebush in full bloom, it's another shot of inspiration. *Hmm... I need to plant another red-flowering plant nearby to create a fabulous color-echo.*

Sometimes success with one plant can be the impetus for an entire border, exactly what happened with when 'Cinco de Mayo' came on the scene. A hardy fuchsia on the opposite end provided not only a nice color to tie it all together but the bulk as well. The rose and the fuchsia were like the bookends with multiple similar-themed books—er, *plants*—between.

But, to be honest, the success of my rose-fuchsia border resulted only after several failed attempts with different plants. I can't even remember all the plants that *didn't* work or all the reasons they didn't. I'm just glad that I eventually—through trial and error—found a design that did.

One of the nice things about gardening is that usually you can amend a border or grouping as needed without too much grief. I've got a Nine Bark shrub that I planted in a full-sun location last spring. One year later, it's obvious that was a huge mistake. The maroon leaves are irreparably sunburned. Fortunately, it's deciduous. I'll dig it up and play Musical Plants until that ah-ha moment occurs—and keep my fingers crossed that next year's leaves look like they're supposed to.

You don't know until you try.

Through the decades of being alive on this earth, I've come to the conclusion that my life—all our lives—are guided by a Creator. When I'm attuned, I can sense a divine presence steering my day-to-day comings and goings. When I'm perceptive, I have the opportunity to gain insight, see my blessings and embrace the learning opportunities.

Much of the time, I admit, I'm not attuned at all. I'm too engrossed in my tangible milieu to think about anything beyond it.

I truly believe that people are a lot like plants.

Some people/plants look handsome and dashing in their pots but when you get too close, you're jabbed by a painful thorn. You back away in an effort to disentangle yourself, all the while hoping the thing doesn't have far-reaching tentacles.

Others, when you read their tag, offer grandiose promises. They grow to maturity in twelve easy months, instantly providing that much-needed protection from the vagaries of summer. You buy their line and plant them, full of hope and happy with their larger-than-life presence in your

garden—but only until it becomes apparent that they suck all the nutrients and moisture and life from everything around them and leave a wasteland in their wake.

Some people/plants are sweet and good natured. You bring Ms. Jovial home and plant her exactly where she wants to be because you're so delighted with the friendship you've formed. But in no time at all, you're in shock and stunned when she has ignored her boundaries, jumped her allotted space and taken over the entire bed with her good-natured disposition.

And some people/plants—most, actually—offer sweet fruit and lovely blossoms. They grow unattended save for your occasional visitation with the watering can. You talk to them and prune them as needed, bring the blossoms inside to perfume the house, and enjoy the nutritious fruit for breakfast. You mulch them well in the winter and they show their appreciation by zipping through unscathed only to grow thicker and more lush the following year. These become your lifelong friends.

I suppose if we didn't have the thorns and the grandiose promises and the boundary-jumpers we wouldn't be able to appreciate the true friends.

Chapter Twenty-Five ~
A Strong Foundation

One of the major tenets of successful gardening is minding the soil. You can't build a beautiful garden if the foundation is weak.

Most plants will perform much better if they're grown in soil that is rich and friable and teeming with microorganisms. I say most because for every rule there is an exception. Desert plants would rot in typical garden soil. They want their roots dry and prefer sandy, arid soil that we call dust. And, on the opposite extreme, there are plants that grow on the riparian shores of lakes and rivers that might wither and die in typical garden soil. They want their roots wet and prefer that waterlogged brown stuff we often call mud.

Gardeners strive for healthy plants. We're driven by a mysterious nurturing urge that causes us to do things that any sane person would think twice about. There are days when, should someone peek over the fence, they'd witness us hauling heavy wheelbarrow-loads of manure or compost or shredded leaves to the farthest reaches of our landscapes where we lovingly spread the organic riches atop the soil. We know that doing this will help our gardens in four important ways. First, as the organic matter breaks down, it will feed the soil's microorganisms which in turn will feed the plants. Second, it will regulate the soil temperature and help insulate plants' root systems from extremes. Third, top dressing the soil will suppress the bane of every gardener: weeds. And fourth, fertile soil will retain moisture more efficiently. Soil won't become overly waterlogged or dry out too quickly.

Some how-to garden books might tell us there are proper times to apply compost and a right and a wrong way to do it. Opposite the detailed instructions, the book will have a full-page glossy photo of a size two model wearing designer gardening clothes, topped with a sun hat, posing with a Revlon-esque face in front of a pristine wheelbarrow fresh from the factory. She looks pretty good, we might think, stifling the urge to perform a brief, self-deprecating assessment of our own worn out body in front of the mirror.

But seasoned gardeners will eschew the well-meant advice from the coffee table tomes and declare that *any time* is the *proper* time to compost. It's when the weather and our schedules cooperate. We compost when we *can*.

I'm writing this in mid-November on a Sunday morning. It's raining and windy and maybe about forty degrees. The last time I was outside, I noticed thousands upon thousands of tiny weed seedlings sprouting all over my garden beds. I shouldn't be sitting on my comfy sofa typing. I should be out there breaking my back to cover and smother those seedlings before they grow and bloom and go to seed and spread that seed all over Timbuktu.

But I'm not. I'm also an eternal optimist and I'm pretty sure a rare sunny day will reveal itself and will be the perfect time. I'll don my non-designer boots and work-worn gloves, grab my leaky, squeaky wheelbarrow, and tackle my task with aplomb. Amazingly, it almost always works this way.

Years ago when I first began my gardening odyssey, I didn't pay much attention to the soil. I wasn't interested in spending my precious dollars on boring things of that nature. Buying plants was a lot more fun. While waiting in line with my basketful of colorful pretties, I'd gaze around at fellow shoppers, their flatbed carts piled high with packaged soil amendments. How pathetic, I'd think, disguising my smarmy attitude with a friendly smile.

I'm not sure exactly when I became interested in compost, but I think it was after attempting to dig a hole to plant one of my purchased beauties only to find a pool of water beneath mucky material that stuck to my shovel and gloves. Or it might have been when I began paying attention to the kitchen scraps I was tossing by the bucketful into what could be loosely defined as a compost bin. Or it might have been after my husband purchased a Ford Ranger pickup and I could beg him to bring me home a yard of compost for twelve bucks from the municipal recycling place.

Yes, I think it was then.

It didn't hurt when my sweet son came over in autumn and tested out his riding lawn mower. Rolling back and forth over the fallen leaves from the three towering sweet gum trees, he then deposited the shredded detritus in a pile for me to spread at my leisure.

By this time I was completely excited bordering on maniacal over the prospect. "My plants will love you for this," I told my son, who seemed very pleased with himself.

It's true. Plants prefer to root themselves in soil that is healthy and fertile. Using organic matter somehow magically—aka scientifically—balances the microscopic playing field and provides a healthy environment for unencumbered growth. Plants will look better, perform better, and be more resistant to bugs and diseases.

I often ponder the parallels between plants and people. If we're provided with a balanced foundation and healthy environment, especially during our formative years, we'll grow and thrive and do what we're supposed to do, unencumbered. But if the foundation is faulty or the environment is missing something or if there is not a proper balance of nurturing and boundaries, we'll be vulnerable to a plethora of pathogens. We'll be weak and brittle until we discover and implement the balance for ourselves.

Chapter Twenty-Six ~ The Hunt

Carol's red Toyota Tacoma pickup turns into the driveway at nine a.m. on the dot. She's always on time. I love that about her. Snatching my jacket, I can hear the crinkling wrappers on the two energy bars I stuffed in my purse. I grab my coffee and refrain from hollering "Goodbye, love you," to my sleeping brood.

Carol's pickup is sparkling, with a tan interior and the smells of leather and fresh coffee. It sits much higher than my little Hyundai so it takes a few seconds to get my bearings. When we planned our outing, we agreed that taking Carol's bigger rig would allow for bigger plant purchases, something all plant-obsessed people will understand.

I buckle in as Carol sips her coffee, then slips the truck into reverse to take us out of the driveway. We're off.

An alliance of caffeine and adrenaline aids our growing anticipation as we curlicue through twenty minutes of back roads. I can't tell whether I'll need my jacket or not with the sun defiantly playing peek-a-boo with the wispy spring clouds.

We talk about our gardens, our families, and current events, until finally the signage we've been looking for comes into view: a nursery tucked secretively within the ubiquitous Douglas firs of western Oregon. These are the best, the ones located smack dab on the owners' land instead of some corner lot in town, the ones that require a bit of purposed navigation and a little help from Google Maps.

We're greeted with a friendly hello and hearty laughter by the owner, who resembles a burly mix of Tom Selleck and Chris Farley. Although we've been here before, we're not exactly best buddies with this guy and the pleasantries feel somewhat contrived, but okay, all things considered. Plant people are almost always congenial.

It doesn't take me long to wrap up the chit-chat. As much as I enjoy the human connection, my attention is focused beyond the checkout pavilion where potted shrubs flow into perennials all neatly soldiered in what must be a few hundred rows that end abruptly at a band of trees at the far end.

Carol and I share a knowing look and a chuckle then begin our jaunt down the widest aisle, avoiding the intermittent puddles that originate from the sprinklers or a recent rain or both. I should have worn better shoes.

As we walk, we discuss the plants we already have and how they're doing. We see plants we've killed and briefly deliberate on whether or not to try them again.

Daphne 'Summer Ice' catches my interest. My plant at home is also blooming and seeing it here offers a subtle confirmation that I did the right thing by choosing it for the spot in which it now thrives. I give myself a mental pat on the back and then bend down to catch a whiff of its delicious perfume—and briefly contemplate on whether I should buy a second plant for another part of the garden. Maybe.

Despite my incessant praises, Carol remains skeptical, having lost several *Daphne odora*. "But this one isn't fussy at all," I insist. But she remains hesitant for reasons only she knows. Plant hunting is exceedingly subjective. Somehow there is an intrinsic *knowing* when a plant wants to come home with you. So far it seems that Daphne and Carol aren't meant to be friends.

I understand, because I'm not exactly fond of the Pieris that Carol swoons over. Pieris, or Andromeda as old-time gardeners sometimes refer to it, is pleasant as it rolls across the tongue—Pee-air-is or An-drom-ih-duh—but to me the pronunciation is where the allure ends. Maybe it's because the poor plant is over-used in municipal landscapes, and often misused, planted in full, scorching sun. Maybe in the right place, I might feel less disapproving. But I'm not going to buy it.

Carol loves Pieris and spends several minutes mulling over a new variety just finishing up its blooming cycle.

Mostly, we're just looking, pricing, moving on. We always start out this way. With a burgeoning mini-nursery at home, being selective is not only prudent, it's a necessity. It's not just the monetary outlay but the nagging question "Where will I plant it?" Having a specific plant in mind for a specific location is always nice, but sometimes the inspiration doesn't happen until we're out there, face to face with all of the options and possibilities.

Oftentimes, if I see a plant I love but don't have a specific spot in my garden for it, I'll rationalize its purchase by telling myself "It'll look nice in a big pot." If the price is right, I'll buy it, bring it home, plant it in said pot, and position it somewhere, depending on its sun/shade requirements.

This container method will work well for the types of plants that can tolerate apartment dwelling, the big city plants, the New Yorkers who are content to put down roots in their limited, allotted space.

But even some of those plants, I've found, eventually crave a different lifestyle. They're tired of the city's confinements and want to stretch out in the country, buy a farm, and live off the land.

My 'Tiger Eyes Sumac' and my Tinkerbell lilac are prime examples. Each has been living in New York City—in a Park Avenue penthouse, judging by the girth of their pots. But in the last few years they haven't been advancing in size as they should be. It's become apparent that I need to find a spot and let them live off the land.

The downside to relocating is finding that perfect spot in a crowded garden, digging a suitably deep hole, and heaving the monster root ball over to the hole. The upside is that I've got an empty penthouse ready for another city dweller.

At the moment, most of the hard work of gardening is sequestered in the back of my mind as I meander down the nursery aisles with my best garden buddy Carol. Right now, it's not about the work—or the play—of gardening. It's about *the hunt,* that primitive compulsion to forage and locate and seize the elusive must-have something-or-other. It goes back multiple generations, perhaps to the cavewoman, stalking the forest in search of sustenance.

And while I have no idea whether cavewomen actually stalked the forest, I do know for certain that a primal adrenaline rush spikes with the discovery and procurement of a coveted specimen. It's addictive and it can often cloud one's better judgment. *Now my garden and my entire life will be absolutely perfect.*

I've been looking down at the immediate offerings in the main aisle for quite some time. To get my bearings, I look up and scan the periphery.

And the alarm sounds. My own personal Pink Alert.

My eyes have homed in on something *pink* in the distance. *Pink.* Anyone who knows my garden proclivities is aware of my shameless passion for pink.

I find the color pink absolutely, undeniably, unarguably, irresistible. And the reasons why remain a mystery, particularly as I don't really fit the profile for a pink person. I'm nobody's girly-girl. It's been years since I've put on a dress, I'm not a romantic, and I rarely cry, but from baby to burgundy, I'm an unapologetic, die-hard pink maniac.

With the Pink Alert fueling my curiosity, I look down, then up, and plot my course to the spot of pink. I launch forward, abandoning Carol who is no doubt rolling her eyes. I practically trip over several errant pots of Echinacea and feel the ice on my toes as I step in a puddle I misjudged as being shallow.

Getting closer, several rows of slender, cascading leaves come in to view. They look suspiciously like the foliage of the Daylily. *Nah. Can't be. Daylilies are dusty-orange, not pink.*

But there they are, those unmistakable stems jutting upwards from the center of those strappy, downward-facing leaves. Each stem carries a few blooms tucked among clusters of buds. And the blooms are definitely pink!

I offer a brief glance and smile back to Carol who is now making her way towards me, wisely avoiding the puddles, parts of which now reside inside my saturated shoes. She's still too far away to talk to without yelling, and since there are several other customers here, I offer a quick wave instead.

I inch forward, careful with my steps as I contend with my hyperactive adrenaline. When I'm close enough, I cup a blossom in my hand. Exquisite. Six soft-pink petals face outward, and a glow from a fairy's tiny lamplight illuminates from deep inside the flower's center. I must be dreaming.

Weak-kneed, I rummage through the foliage of several plants, looking for a label. "Hemerocallis 'Coming Up Roses'" is scribbled across a narrow, dirty tag. I read it out loud to Carol who has just arrived to see what all the fuss is about.

"A pink daylily? Did you know they came in pink?" I ask an equally incredulous Carol.

"No," she says, shaking her head and walking down the narrow aisle to find her own specimen.

"Coming Up Roses," I say quietly once more. Such an endearing moniker. Truthfully, this Daylily could be identified as 'Mud With A Mix of Dung' and it wouldn't matter. Seeing is believing, and I believe this beauty needs to come home with me.

Up until that moment, I've never been a huge fan of the Daylily. Too often I see them neglected. Without regular maintenance, the plant can look haggard and pathetic with day-old—and older—blossoms hanging flaccidly above the clump of narrow leaves that always seem to be a mixture of healthy green and tired brown. And I can't say I've been the least bit thrilled with the blossom colors. Orange and yellow look great in other gardens, but they don't belong in mine.

Taking my cues from Carol, I stand and scan the row, looking for the 'Coming Up Roses' Daylily with the most buds. I want my plant to be in bloom for as long as possible.

I bring home my treasure and a few other must-haves and embark on some serious Musical Plants to accommodate them. And the bliss multiplies: this discovery had opened my eyes. They were real.

Eventually, two more pink daylily cultivars found their way into my heart and my garden. Each blooms at a slightly different time during the summer, which prolongs the display.

That day, this cavewoman had been very successful with her hunt.

Chapter Twenty-Seven ~ Vulnerabilities

Non-gardeners need to know that we who take gardening seriously are a quirky bunch. For one thing, we're never satisfied. We're always pulled towards new plants and are always fine tuning our gardens' borders. It can be very difficult for us to just relax and enjoy beauty we create.

I go through gardening phases. I'll form a bright vision for one aspect of gardening and it will dull all other aspects, sort of like a tunnel vision trance. If it's a new plant genus I'm interested in, I'll research the genus thoroughly and whether they'll grow in my garden. For me, it's a highly fulfilling way to enjoy my hobby ... and I sort of can't help myself.

Several years ago I began my Reading-Garden-Books-in-Earnest phase/obsession. While heaving a roughly fifty pound bag of garden tomes onto the library's checkout counter, I'd avoid eye contact with the genteel librarian and attempt small talk through nervous laughter, hoping that my obvious obsession wouldn't cause her to judge me too harshly.

As I pored over the stack of garden books perched on my nightstand, I discovered that many of the authors, in an effort to educate the reader, would elaborate on a plant and all its attributes including where it originated. In other words, details *ad nauseam* about where intrepid plant explorers of yesteryear such as David Douglas or Robert Fortune had discovered the plant growing in the wild. How they either dug it up or gathered seeds or severed a bunch of branches to bring back to the Royal Horticultural Society of England or whatever organization had sponsored the expedition. It seemed like a bunch of useless information to me. I didn't need to read about the plant's history to be convinced of its merit. I felt as though the author was trying to wow me with vast academic research and I wasn't impressed. It was the here-and-now I was interested in. I wanted to know how the plant was used in the author's garden and whether or not it would survive in mine.

Eventually, as my obsession mellowed from mania to moderation, it dawned on me that what I had assumed was the author's excessive pedagogy was actually a more thorough explanation of the plant's needs. I began to see that if I understood the setting in nature where the plant thrived, I would know what kind of environment to replicate in my own garden for the plant's success. I'm a little ashamed of my impatience and for judging the authors harshly.

So I decided to try out this principle with Salvias, a fairly easy group of plants to grow in the garden. I'd had success with several varieties but felt a pull towards the fancy-schmancy *Salvia pachyphylla*. This particular species really made me salivate with its thick, pinky-purple blooming spires above aromatic, gray foliage. From my reading, I discovered that it grew wild in the arid hills of California, Nevada, and Arizona. Barring a miracle, this plant probably wouldn't survive the wet winters and muddy soil of my western Oregon garden, at least not without some serious intervention on my part. I would have to do everything I could think of to mimic those arid hills.

I plopped not one but two three-inch tall plants in my arid rock garden. And there they sat. And there they *still* sit. In all this time, they haven't grown at all. They haven't died, either, which I suppose says something.

Clearly, I didn't quite replicate the perfect environment for my little charges.

Plan B, which is code for Last Ditch, is to dig them up and put them in a container that I can move around in hopes of finding a spot that does a slightly better job of mimicking their native habitat.

Some plants, unlike the aforementioned Salvia, are highly adaptable to different conditions. Purple Coneflower, for instance. Because it grows wild in much of the eastern United States, it will adapt to many different garden situations—unless your garden is located in deep shade. Adaptability only goes so far.

For several years I went through a phase where all the plants I was interested in obtaining were rare and hard to find. I'd read about them, completely entranced by their structure, foliage, and flower. Then I'd search through my mail order catalogs hoping to find a decently priced specimen. Most times the price and the cost of having it shipped, which was often nearly as much as the cost of the plant, forestalled my purchase. Needing to do *something*, I'd add the must-have plant to my wish list and hope that at some point the local retailers would have it in stock. Many times, by waiting a few years, I was pleasantly surprised to find what I wanted locally. Patience is indeed a virtue, especially where the ol' wallet is concerned.

Patience would also have been helpful while I was in the midst of my fragrance phase, but as I am so often wont to do, I ignored that caution. My garden was already crammed full of horticultural wonders, but no matter. I was focused on searching out pleasingly aromatic plants to add, and I'd find room, somewhere, by golly.

One of the plants I was enchanted with was Pineapple Broom. I read that it produced yellow, Lupine-shaped flowers that emitted a perfume reminiscent of fresh pineapple. I was willing to waive my ban on yellow flowers just once to accommodate this beauty. Like some weird cosmic game of tag, the harder I searched for it, the more convinced I was that I had to have it. When I finally located it at a nursery in Eugene, about forty miles south, I got in the car and made the trip.

Upon arriving, I sought out nursery personnel because the grounds were huge and I didn't want to waste countless hours wandering all over trying to find my beloved Pineapple Broom. I could do that after I had my coveted specimen in my cart.

A nice-looking young man offered to assist me. He appeared knowledgeable, but, to my surprise, he wasn't familiar with Pineapple anything. I was beginning to wonder if he thought I was trying to trick him so I grabbed my tattered catalog and shoved it towards him. "Seeeee" I said, pointing a worried finger at the documented mystery plant.

After following the poor guy through row upon row of potted plants, we, at long last, found it. I stared at it with labored enthusiasm as nagging doubts engulfed me. The plant just wasn't all that impressive. I fought back the urge to tell him that I had changed my mind, but I didn't dare. I knew that as soon as I got home I'd regret deciding not to buy it. I paid him and spent another hour looking around, then drove home happy. Sort of.

Unfortunately, it didn't take long to see that although the flowers were unique and admittedly stunning, the fragrance was miniscule. And the plant grew too tall to deadhead effectively, which meant brown, desiccated protrusions atop the gray, felted foliage. Dead-brown and felted gray don't exactly make for a harmonious color scheme. I cut the whole bush down and it promptly died of rejection, which really wasn't my intention. Really. I suppose the lesson here is that maybe some plants are rare for a reason.

I've done a lot of thinking on that subject. Maybe the things we read about and convince ourselves we want or need aren't really all they're cracked up to be. Maybe the prose we're reading is more hype than truth. I'm not faulting the authors of the garden books. Usually they're honest about a plant's attributes and shortcomings because they don't have an agenda. And a lot of times plant failures are due to human error, of which I'm guilty. And maybe I just bought an inferior plant.

But what about advertisers in general? They have an agenda. And science and well-planned strategies behind what they do. People fall for it all the time.

I think one of the traps we're vulnerable to is believing there is a hole in our lives that only a certain product can fill. Of course, the advertisers aren't going to come right out and say, "Your life sucks and you need my product to make it fabulous." They're much too smart for that. They know exactly how to appeal to our desires with flowery prose and pretty pictures meticulously designed to convince us of our *need* for their products.

Too many times I've succumbed to that compulsion to buy something, be it a plant or a candy bar, just because I think it will make my life better. I need to stop that. I need to step back and analyze what I'm doing and let my decision be based on logic rather than unchecked emotion.

That doesn't mean I'm never going to buy another plant, just that I'm aware of the fact that I'm vulnerable to the advertisers. I think on some level, in some way, we all are.

Chapter Twenty-Eight ~
Healthy Escapism

Years ago, I read that gardeners, whether aware of it or not, attempt to mimic special places they enjoyed during childhood.

The silver lining to an otherwise unhealthy upbringing was that my siblings and I were able to spend a good deal of our time outdoors. Our river property in southern Oregon was incredibly beautiful with gnarly, lichen-encrusted Oak trees huddled like teammates strategizing their next move. The understory was ankle-high grass that would turn tawny every July. The North Umpqua River was blue and friendly, endlessly gurgling over and around smooth rocks and water grasses. In winter, the trees were barren save for clusters of mistletoe sequestered high on their branches like trapped tumbleweed, and the river, once blue and inviting, became hot cocoa complete with marshmallows in the form of runaway logs bobbing up and down as they moved downstream and out of sight. After the bus driver dropped us off at the intersection of North Bank Road and Echo Drive, then effortlessly turned her bus around to head back to the school, miles away, I'd hurry inside to watch the river from the living room windows.

Our nearest neighbor, Mr. Gordon, was a gardener ahead of his time. While the other lots sported no-nonsense driveways carved in the paths of least resistance from road to house, his wove and wound around shrubs and trees, back and forth before ending at the parking area by the house. It was as if Mr. Gordon intended his guests to visit the garden before visiting the people.

Once, when the school bus broke down, Mrs. Gordon drove us home in her little VW Bug. That was the only time I traveled the curvy driveway. It was magical.

The Gordons were unique people. They had a pair of caged squirrel monkeys in their living room. Mrs. Gordon liked to make fabric dyes out of plants. Their daughter had toys that made me sick with envy. Her miniature furniture and accessories would have made Barbie salivate.

Mr. Gordon had the face of Glenn Ford. Even at the nascent age of eight I could see the resemblance. He was formidable and I was terrified of him, as I was with all adults. Once when my father was using his chainsaw to bring the logs down and sever them into woodstove-size, which he then forced his children to stack, Mr. Gordon stood outside by his house and watched. I felt he was attempting to telepathically communicate his annoyance with my father's deafening chainsaw. My father, of course, ignored him.

Mr. Gordon created a natural-looking creek by using water pumped from the river through buried pipe. It started at the top of the property and meandered alongside the driveway, then along one side of the house, down the embankment and eventually back to the river.

My sisters, brother, and I played with the Gordon's daughter in a sandy area just before the creek waters reunited with the river. We'd build our sand-houses on the creek's shores, find little stones for cars, and break off the tips of shrubs to poke in the sand for trees. We'd see tadpoles, an occasional frog, and once we found a small turtle. Even then, I knew I was on sacred ground. It was as if the skies had opened and the Creator had lowered a bit of heaven for us traumatized kids to enjoy.

I avoid the temptation to grab on to something new. I don't even get enthused about Christmas until a week or so before the actual day. I need time to let ideas simmer before I open the lid and take a bite. So it wasn't until garden water features had become pretty standard fare that I got on board and decided to create one in my garden. I knew exactly what I wanted. But I was still not a lottery winner and I'd lost touch with the Gordons decades ago. I had to settle for what I could afford and create on my own.

My garden has three ponds, although one of them barely qualifies since it's small and shallow, more like a large water bowl below ground level.

Surprisingly, not long after I dug and installed my ponds, tadpoles arrived from out of nowhere. This was, of course, after the raccoons invited their relatives over for one of their midnight soirees where they dined on the brightly colored goldfish my daughters and I had purchased at the pet store. Since raccoons don't seem to have a taste for tadpoles, they escaped the slaughter and are now a regular fixture in the garden

Around the first part of March, the croaking begins in earnest. It's noticeable all day, but gets quite deafening around dusk. I can hear them from the kitchen. I'll walk outside and all goes silent, which I assume means they're either catching their breath or trying to discern whether I'm a threat. A few minutes later, they'll resume their chorus. That seems to alert the frogs in the other pond to join in. And so it goes, back and forth like a well-timed echo. But frogs are not patient and don't always wait for a reply. They seem to enjoy arguing and hearing their own croaks. Sometimes as many as six of them will croak simultaneously and I can hear my eardrums rattle.

I've always felt a weird need to apologize to the neighbors for this backyard cacophony that comes dangerously close to breaking the neighborhood noise ordinance.

I still haven't had a turtle visitor, but that's okay. It's the idea of having life-giving water that counts. How serene and soothing it is to hear the trickle of water as it splashes on the rocks. How delightful to see blue sky mirrored on the water's surface or moonlight reflected off the ripples of the little fountain I installed all by myself. And, as annoying as it can sometimes become, listening to the frogs as they express their delight with life is extremely gratifying. I love that I've created an environment that lures critters from afar and makes them feel safe enough to take up residence.

Although my adult life is infinitely less stressful than my childhood was, my need to be outdoors didn't end when I grew up. My creativity, once centered on sand-houses and searching for turtles, only grew more sophisticated with my love of garden design and plant care. Deep down, I'm still that kid getting a thrill over hearing a frog or seeing a butterfly or a pretty plant combination.

I believe all gardeners would agree that nature is a great escape from the rigors of life for people of all ages. Often when I've had a stressful day and my head is full of conflict, I can escape to nature, just as I did when I was a kid. I can feel the quickening of the pleasure sensor in my brain as it releases its relaxing elixir to drown out those pesky quandaries. Suddenly I'm not fretting any longer.

I think it's important to give our busy, stressed minds a break, either through a hobby or a good book or movie. Like a gentle breeze clears away the fog, we'll be rejuvenated and able to see the bigger picture. We'll be better equipped to tackle our goals, and able to endure life's responsibilities for another day.

Chapter Twenty-Nine ~ The Garden is Never Finished

The orange cord looks like a spray painted snake sprawled across the lawn. It slithers along the pathway and climbs up the stairs to the handy outdoor outlet. A large middle section of it is still bundled together to curtail the chaotic tangle that would ensue should I set it entirely free. I consider it my avoidance of operator error, or, better yet, operator impatience. Rolling up a forty-foot power cord isn't exactly my forte. My arms aren't long enough.

At my end of the snake is the foreboding, equally cautionary orange, electric hedge trimmer. I began using it when the motor on my manual hedge trimmer—me—wore out. It was the constant bending that did it. Well, that and the habitual back and forth arm movement. Plus the blades got dull and rusty. And my son found a brand new electric hedge trimmer at a garage sale. With all of these reasons, in addition to the fact that I didn't want to hurt his feelings, I felt compelled to give it a try.

The hedge in need of a trim is *Lonicera nitida,* an evergreen shrub with tiny, dark green leaves and a penchant for fast growth and easy rooting. The common name is Box Honeysuckle, but only because it's from the same genus as the common honeysuckle. The teensy spring-blooming flowers are a magnet for bees but a little too small for human enjoyment.

Motivated by an overabundance of caution, I set my hands in their proper positions, mindful that if I don't I could lose a finger, or worse. My eyes do a quick scan to confirm that the orange snake is a safe distance from the sharp protrusion of the trimmer. Check. With a slight trigger-pull, the rattly *brr* begins in earnest, obliterating birdsong and the occasional croak of a tree frog, and bigger sounds, like the telephone ringing or a sonic jet flying over.

The manual hedge trimmer only made a small, *swish-click* sound and an occasional operator groan.

Another annoying characteristic of the orange tyrant is how it shakes semi-violently—unless you're the plant, for whom it is *exceptionally* violent—while I hold it. As soon as I let my finger relax, the rattling ceases, and I hear the birds again. My arms and hands tingle and I need to shake them to relieve my quivering, overly vibrated muscles.

I start it up once again and run the oscillating blades across my hedge. The result is instant neatness. The job is finished in minutes, and, as I whisper a prayer of thanks that I didn't lose a limb, I disentangle the snake so I can fold it up and stuff it out of sight once more. I am still left with gathering and disposing of an ocean of little hedge trimmings, but who can argue with such a quick spruce-up, particularly of such a fast grower. And by fast I mean overnight. If I had the patience, I could probably sit in my Adirondack chair and watch those little severed ends jut upwards, measuring the inches by minutes. But I'm not patient. I have other tasks waiting to get done.

Although it's efficient, I enjoy using the electric hedge trimmer about as much as I enjoy running into a cloud of hungry mosquitoes, which is to say *I don't.*

Partly it's that I, generally speaking, loathe power tools. I like the old fashioned way of doing things: manually. I'm an idealist that way, relegating the appropriate muscles to do the work rather than the counterfeit muscles that require a monthly sum of my hard-earned money. I'm an idealist and also a hypocrite. As much as I despise the noise and the bother of twenty-first century yard and garden contrivances readily available at the nearest Big Box, I appreciate what results when they're employed. The instant gratification of going from jungle to English Estate Garden is exhilarating.

***

Several years ago, while perusing the library's garden section, I stumbled upon *Growing Pains: Time and Change in the Garden* by Patricia Thorpe. Although I was somewhat worried about the bad news I was going to encounter in this book, I brought it home and tried to dive in. But the waters were icy and foreboding, with currents that I was sure I couldn't quite navigate. In other words, the book contained a message I didn't want to embrace. The author discussed the challenges of having a mature garden and the need for constant maintenance and perhaps the need to rethink things. Because my garden was young and growing, I couldn't relate to issues such as overgrown masses and narrow pathways.

Now, at this stage of my gardening career and the current state of my garden, I think I could probably benefit from reading Ms. Thorpe's book. My desire for abundance has come back to bite me.

The living garden is always in flux. Even though at times, such as during the winter months, the fluctuations can be microscopic, they happen daily as the growing cycle continues its never ending rotation of budding new leaves and shedding old ones. The only finished garden is one that never changes.

Our job as caretakers of the never-finished garden implies one thing: we're never finished either. We might get the leaves scooped out of the pond before a downpour or get the entire load of compost spread before dark or get the perennials divided and replanted before the weekend is over. We'll hang up our gloves, shake off our garden clogs, and retreat indoors to grab a bite and take a hot bath. But tomorrow there will be a new round of tasks to be tackled. It's an ongoing process.

Maybe the garden knows this. Maybe it's smarter than we think and a tiny bit manipulative. Maybe it enjoys entertaining us as we wander its paths with our clippers and visions. Maybe it suffers from loneliness when we're not in its midst, tending it. Maybe it has an agenda, budding, expanding and dropping its leaves and sprouting little interlopers so we'll stick around and scratch its back, massage its feet and give it a much needed haircut.

Maybe the garden has a toddler mentality, like the little sweetie pie seated in her high chair who drops her spoon on the floor so someone will pick it up and give it back to her so she can drop it again ... and again.

Maybe the garden is engaged in some sort of cunning play with us, causing little bits of chaos here and there. We just keep picking up the clippers because we possess an unwavering need to tidy things up, to keep order and right the wrongs, if not for the world at large, at least for the little world we call a garden.

Life itself is a lot like a garden. It's a never ending cycle of tasks and appointments, earning and spending, sleeping and waking, emptying and filling, talking and listening. It operates as an undulating continuum that will reach heights of breathtaking beauty and lows of heartbreaking anguish. But it must be this way because the alternative is a stagnant, inactive cesspool of death and decay. If we aren't actively using our brains and muscles, we will atrophy.

And this brings me my final point. Although I'm unable to attribute this quote to the wise soul who penned it, I believe it is true.

The garden that is finished is dead.

So, as you don your garden boots and zip up your jacket or slather on the sunscreen and grab your straw hat, remember that today is a good day. The garden eagerly awaits your loving attention and will provide you with satisfaction, heartbreak, frustration and delight—and that's just in the first few minutes. Ultimately, you can be assured that you'll receive the very finest that nature has to offer.

Go little book, and wish to all
Flowers in the garden, meat in the hall,
A bin of wine, spice to wit,
A house with a lawn enclosing it,
A living river by the door
A nightingale in the sycamore.

~Robert Lewis Stevenson (*Underwoods 1887*)

Appendix ~ Latin and Common Name of Referenced Plants

Latin Name	Common Name
Acer circinatum	Maple, vine
Acer macrophyllum	Maple, Big Leaf
Acer palmatum 'Sango Kaku'	Maple, Japanese,
	Maple, Coral Bark
Aegopodium podagraria 'Variegatum'	Variegated Bishop's Weed
Agave attenuata	Agave
Ailanthus altissima	Tree of Heaven
Ajuga reptans	Bugleweed
Aleurites moluccanus	Kukui, Candlenut
Ananas comosus	Pineapple
Anthurium andraeanum	Anthiriums,
	Flamingo Flower
Arbutus unedo 'Compacta'	Dwarf Strawberry
	Tree
Argyrocytisus battandieri	Pineapple Broom
Artemesia ludoviciana 'Silver Queen'	Mugwort
Aster spp.	Michaelmas Daisy
Carica papaya	Papaya
Casuarinae quisetifolia	Ironwood Tree
Centaurea montana	Perennial Bachelor Button
Ceratostigma plumbaginoides	Plumago
Choisya ternata	Mexican Orange
Citrus aurantifolia	Lime, Lime tree
Clematis spp., cvs.	Clematis
Cocos nucifera	Coconuts, palm tree
Cosmos bipinnatus	Cosmos
Cyclamen hederafolium	Cyclamen
Daphne odora 'Aureomarginata'	Variegated Winter
	Daphne
Daphne x transatlantica 'Summer Ice'	Daphne
Delphinium spp., cvs.	Delphinium
Echinacea purpurea	Purple coneflower

Euphorbia cyparissias 'Fens Ruby'	Cypress Spurge
Foeniculum vulgare 'Purpureum'	Bronze Fennel
Fuchsia spp., cvs.	Fuchsia
Hakonechloa macra 'Albo Striata'	Japanese Forest Grass
Hemerocallis 'Coming Up Roses'	Daylily
Hibiscus rosa-sinensis	Hibiscus
Hosta plantaginea	Hosta, Plaintain Lily
Indigofera heterantha	Indigo Bush, Himalayan Indigo
Lantana camara	Lantana
Laurentia fluviatilis	Blue Star Creeper
Lavendula spp.	Lavender
Leucanthemum vulgare	Daisy, Oxeye
Liquidambar styraciflua	Sweet Gum Tree
Lonicera japonica 'Halliana'	Hall's Honeysuckle
Lonicera nitida	Boxleaf Honeysuckle
Loropetalum chinensis	Fringe Flower
Lupinus perennis	Lupine
Lysimachia nummularia	Creeping Jenny
Lythrum salicaria	Purple Loosestrife
Mentha citrata	Orange Mint, Bergamot Mint
Monstera deliciosa	Split leaf philodendron
Nandina domestica	Heavenly Bamboo
Penstemon barbatus 'Elfin Pink'	Penstemon 'Elfin Pink'
Phlox paniculata	Garden Phlox
Phormium tenax	New Zealand Flax
Physocarpus opufolius 'Coppertina'	Ninebark
Polygonatum biflorum	Solomon's Seal
Pieris japonica	Andromeda, Lily of the Valley Shrub
Plumeria alba	Frangipani, Plumeria
Prunus laurocerasus	English Laurel
Pseudotsuga menziesii	Douglas Fir Tree
Pyrus communis	Pear Tree
Rosa 'Carpet Rose'	Carpet Rose
Rosa 'Cecile Brunner'	Cecile Brunner Rose
Rosa 'Cinco de Mayo'	Cinco de Mayo Rose

Rosa 'Golden Showers'	Golden Showers Rose
Rosa 'Knock Out'	Knock Out Rose
Rosa mutabilis	Mutabalis Rose
Rhus tphynia 'Tiger Eyes'	Sumac, Tiger Eyes
Rubus armeniacus	Blackberry, Himalayan
Rubus cvs.	Raspberry Plants
Rudbeckia hirta	Black Eyed Susans
Rhododendron spp.	Azalea
Sagina subulata	Scotch moss
Salvia pachyphylla	Mojave Sage, Mountain Desert Sage
Solanum lycopersicum var. cerasiforme	Cherry tomato 'Sweet 100'
Syringa meyeri x microphylla 'Tinkerbell'	Lilac
Tagetes patula	Marigolds
Tanacetum partenium 'Plenum'	Feverfew
Taxus baccata	Yew

About the Author

Grace Peterson divides her time between working as an administrative assistant, writing, and gardening. In addition to being a staff member of The Memoir Writers Society, she authors two blogs, and writes a newspaper garden column for *Northwest Boomer & Senior News*. Her stories can be found in several anthologies. Her memoir, *Reaching*, was awarded the gold standard of literary excellence by Princeton Literary Review.

Grace is the proud mother of four grown children, four friendly felines, and has been married to her best friend since 1980. She lives in western Oregon.

Please visit her blogs, *Subplots by Grace* for "weekly posts about current events, writer and author information, and whatever is on my mind." at www.gracepete.com, and *Gardening With Grace* where she shares "brief discussions with ample photos of my garden's current state" at www.gracepete.blogspot.com

ALSO BY GRACE PETERSON

GRACE PETERSON

REACHING

a memoir

Grace's turbulent childhood, with father's violent temper and mother's apathy, their divorce, and her relocation with her mother and siblings to Hawaii, where she experiences racism and violence, sets the stage for this incredible real-life tale of abuse, brainwashing, and ~ ultimately ~ the long journey to recovery.

At seventeen, Grace experiences love for the first time, but is soon unable contain the traumas of her past. Seeking a remedy from what she perceives as a spiritual problem, she enlists the aid of Brock, a charismatic exorcist and cult expert. Grace stumbles into a world of esoteric rituals, Luciferian doctrines, and New World Order conspiracies.

This gripping narrative illustrates how children adapt to a hostile environment, can grow up misreading their untreated traumas, and, while searching for answers, fall prey to unscrupulous charlatans who heap more damage onto an already wounded soul.

PRAISE FOR *REACHING*

....In short, this is an astonishingly well-sculpted book that reveals Peterson to be a wordsmith on a par with the finest. This is not meant to negate the importance of the message of the book: this is one of the most sincerely penetrating memoirs of a child's journey through a jungle of problems to reach adulthood and become a symbol of the growth that is possible even in the most impossible of histories. In art this is called Form Follows Function, and a finer compliment for a book, especially a memoir, could not be made.

~Grady Harp, Amazon Top 50 Reviewer

Kudos, first to Grace for finding her way through the labyrinth of her life to emerge like the mighty Phoenix from the ashes. What a heroic journey! Along the way Grace found her voice. That is great news for the rest of us! She's a gifted author with a commanding use of language. I have just finished listening to the well-done audiobook version, highly recommend this format.

~Barbara Woolley, author of *Out of the Box: A Soul's Surprising Journey*

Reaching is the gut wrenching story of a girl growing up without love, warmth, or care from her parents and other adults in her life. They were so isolated from each other that the girl called them the mother, the father, the scary aunt, the mean grandmother. The neglect that characterized her young life broke my heart and compelled me to keep reading in hopes that her life would get better.

Throughout, the main character's voice was raw, open, and courageous. This is a book that is brutally honest and beautifully written. I'll never forget it.

~Madeline40

ALL THINGS THAT MATTER PRESS

FOR MORE INFORMATION ON TITLES AVAILABLE FROM
ALL THINGS THAT MATTER PRESS, GO TO
http://allthingsthatmatterpress.com
or contact us at
allthingsthatmatterpress@gmail.com

CPSIA information can be obtained
at www.ICGtesting.com
Printed in the USA
LVHW042348280322
714617LV00019B/2253